DATE DUE

DEMCO 38-296

NEWS & NEWSMAKING

NEWS &
NEWSMAKING

Essays by
Stephen Hess

The Brookings Institution
Washington, D.C.

n Data

Hess, Stephen.
    News & Newsmaking /essays by Stephen Hess.
        p.   cm.
    Includes bibliographical references and index.
    ISBN 0-8157-3634-7 (cloth) —ISBN 0-8157-3633-9 (pbk.)
    1. Press and politics—United States. 2. Journalists—Washington
(D.C) 3. Government and the press—United States. I. Title.
PN4888.P6H49 1995
071'.3—dc20   95-41745
                                                                  CIP

9 8 7 6 5 4 3 2 1

The paper used in this publication meets the minimum requirements
of the American National Standard for Information Sciences—
Permanence of Paper for Printed Library Materials,
ANSI Z39.48-1984.

Typeset in Bembo and Helvetica Condensed

Composition by AlphaTechnologies/mps, Inc.
Charlotte Hall, Maryland

Printed by R.R. Donnelley and Sons Co.
Harrisonburg, Virginia

THE BROOKINGS INSTITUTION

The Brookings Institution is an independent organization devoted to nonpartisan research, education, and publication in economics, government, foreign policy, and the social sciences generally. Its principal purposes are to aid in the development of sound public policies and to promote public understanding of issues of national importance.

The Institution was founded on December 8, 1927, to merge the activities of the Institute for Government Research, founded in 1916, the Institute of Economics, founded in 1922, and the Robert Brookings Graduate School of Economics and Government, founded in 1924.

The Board of Trustees is responsible for the general administration of the Institution, while the immediate direction of the policies, program, and staff is vested in the President, assisted by an advisory committee of the officers and staff. The by-laws of the Institution state: "It is the function of the Trustees to make possible the conduct of scientific research, and publication, under the most favorable conditions, and to safeguard the independence of the research staff in the pursuit of their studies and in the publication of the results of such studies. It is not a part of their function to determine, control, or influence the conduct of particular investigations or the conclusions reached."

The President bears final responsibility for the decision to publish a manuscript as a Brookings book. In reaching his judgment on the competence, accuracy, and objectivity of each study, the President is advised by the director of the appropriate research program and weighs the views of a panel of expert outside readers who report to him in confidence on the quality of the work. Publication of a work signifies that it is deemed a competent treatment worthy of public consideration but does not imply endorsement of conclusions or recommendations.

The Institution maintains its position of neutrality on issues of public policy in order to safeguard the intellectual freedom of the staff. Hence interpretations or conclusions in Brookings publications should be understood to be solely those of the authors and should not be attributed to the Institution, to its trustees, officers, or other staff members, or to the organizations that support its research.

Foreword

As Stephen Hess starts his twenty-fifth year as a senior fellow at Brookings, we are pleased to publish two volumes of his essays about the institutions that have been the primary focus of his research here, *Presidents & the Presidency* and *News & Newsmaking*.

The American research organization or think tank, of which Brookings is one of the oldest, has a role without precedent in other countries of serving as a way station between periods of government service for some people or for others as a stop before returning to academia. This role encourages the interchange of ideas between those who practice and those who research public policy and produces a steady stream of analyses and recommendations based on experience and study.

The author's career illustrates one of these patterns. He came to Brookings after concluding two assignments for President Nixon, first as deputy assistant for urban affairs, serving in the White House as chief of staff to Daniel Patrick Moynihan, and then as the national chairman of the White House Conference on Children and Youth. Previously he had been a fellow at Harvard's Institute of Politics and a speechwriter for President Eisenhower.

While at Brookings Mr. Hess has engaged in both research and policy application. He has served as U.S. delegate to the UN General

Assembly in New York, U.S. delegate to the UNESCO General Conference in Paris, as the editor-in-chief of a national Republican platform, and as an adviser to the Carter administration on the structuring of the Executive Office of the President. He has also served on the Washington, D.C., board of higher education, which created the University of the District of Columbia during his tenure, and as chairman of a commission that assisted in reordering government from an appointed to an elected city council.

Brookings scholars are encouraged to test their ideas in the classroom as well. Mr. Hess taught courses on the interaction between government and the media at the John F. Kennedy School at Harvard and at Johns Hopkins University in Baltimore. At the University of Southern California in Los Angeles he created a course on the presidency using tapes of interviews he had conducted with presidential assistants who dated back to Franklin Roosevelt's administration.

The essays in this volume are collected to give the reader a window into the author's approach to research and problem solving and a feel for the Washington that has been his venue during a challenging and sometimes dramatic era.

Publication of these essays has been supported by a grant from the Cissy Patterson Trust and a Goldsmith Research Award from the Joan Shorenstein Center of Harvard University.

The manuscript benefited from the critiques of Thomas E. Mann and Bruce K. MacLaury; from the administrative support of Cynthia Terrels, Inge Lockwood, and Susan A. Stewart; and from the research assistance of Fawn Johnson. The pages were proofread by Ellen Garshick, and Julia Petrakis compiled the index. The book was edited by James R. Schneider, who has worked with Mr. Hess for more than a decade.

The views expressed in these essays are those of the author and should not be ascribed to the trustees, officers, or other staff members of the Brookings Institution.

December 1995   Michael H. Armacost
Washington, D.C.   *President*

Contents

Author's Note

The essays in this volume have been revised since their initial publication, but no consistent or wide-ranging attempt has been made to update the observations. In addition, in the interests of readability for wider audiences, the scholarly footnotes that accompanied most of the essays at their first publication have been dropped. Those readers who are interested in checking sources should consult the version of the essay cited at the bottom of each opening page.

Preface:
A Journey
in Research

The year was 1977. I had said all I thought I had to say about the presidency and was seeking another public policy institution to study. And there it was, the Washington press corps everywhere I looked; and in journalistic terms it was a beat not very well covered.

Most of what had been written about Washington journalism was in the form of reporters' memoirs, the sort of books that should be titled *Presidents Who Have Known Me*. Prototypically was *Six Presidents, Too Many Wars*, by Bill Lawrence, who had covered the White House for the *New York Times* and ABC, and in 1972 told us that chief executives from Franklin Roosevelt through Richard Nixon called him Bill. The most substantial book on the subject, *The Washington Correspondents*, had been Leo C. Rosten's 1936 Ph.D. dissertation from the University of Chicago. There was something refreshing about finding a field to investigate that did not require half a lifetime to catch up on "the literature."

Trying to understand journalists was an initially unnerving experience for someone who had never been one or studied journalism. Who were these strangers? How did they think of themselves and their jobs? How could I test the validity of what they were telling me? Thanks to a small grant that Fred Friendly and Robert Goldmann secured for me from the Ford Foundation, I was able to spend

some months talking with Washington reporters; after 150 interviews, I wrote a paper of hunches about what made them tick: when
and with whom they competed; when and with whom they coop-
erated; what they fought about with their editors; and if they ever
won. Then I imposed on Joseph Albright, Charles Bailey, Robert
Boyd, Peter Braestrup, David Broder, Andrew Glass, Bernard Kalb,
Marvin Kalb, Alan Otten, Richard Reeves, Eileen Shanahan, Hugh
Sidey, Warren Weaver, Robert Zelnick, and other news veterans. "I
have not pulled back from stating impressions that I am well aware
may prove to be wrong. Tell me," I said. They corrected my errors
and I set out to study these journalists in depth.

I quickly learned that Washington reporters do not sit around
talking about the deeper meaning of journalism. Questions to them
on such abstractions were not going to produce much of interest.
These are workers who think in the concrete. So I borrowed a
research design from a company that asks Americans to keep diaries
of what they are watching on TV. The seven-day diary that I sent
reporters in 1978 left spaces for them to track the stories they were
working on (Monday through Sunday), events attended, documents
used, types of sources interviewed. This produced a lot of very
specific information. At the same time, I and my research assistants
did a content analysis of stories that appeared in newspapers and on
television. By looking at what went into the making of Washington
stories and what resulted, we discovered, for example, that many
presidency stories—"President to Ask for Tax Cut in State of
Union"—were actually routed through Congress, especially via
congressional staff members, who knew a lot about presidents and
were delighted to share with reporters. Judging from the types of
sources that reporters listed, the denizens of Capitol Hill were a
more significant force in shaping news than was visible in the final
product, a conclusion that could only have been reached by using
two very different types of research tools.

Incidentally, this exercise taught me a valuable lesson: offer
sources confidentiality *only* on demand. Trying to increase the return
rate on my survey, I sent each reporter a packet consisting of the
diary (to be filled out anonymously), a stamped return envelope, and
an order form to get a free copy of the book. Most reporters returned
the no-name diary along with the book form that identified them in

the same envelope. This was not entrapment. They could have used two envelopes. They simply did not care if their answers remained anonymous (or they cared less than the cost of a postage stamp). I had offered more confidentiality than was necessary, a mistake, by the way, often made by Washington reporters.

I also conducted a telephone survey with the help of a wonderful group of college interns. The primary advantage of this research technique is that a lot of data can be gathered quickly because information can be filled in on a coding sheet. "Of your three closest friends in Washington (excluding your family), how many are journalists?" The answer, nearly half, was an important clue to the inbred nature of Washington reporters. (In other cities, where journalists are fewer, they are less likely to stand apart.)

There are times, of course, when research tools fail. We asked reporters about what future assignments they wanted—a way for us to establish a hierarchy of Washington news beats—but they would not play our game. Many simply replied, "My present job." What to do? We concluded that there is an informal seniority system in the news business. Young reporters are usually given the least desirable assignments. As they gather experience, and as openings develop, they transfer to jobs that they find more congenial. We therefore worked out rankings by looking at the ages of reporters on each beat. (The State Department assignment turned out to have the greatest prestige; the least, number thirteen, was regional reporting, that is, covering a city or state congressional delegation.) My education had begun. And among the early lessons were: invent, borrow, or adapt research tools that give you the best chance of producing useful information; and the more types of research tools you use, the more apt you are to arrive at a rounded picture.

All this research went into a book called *The Washington Reporters* (1981). Next I wanted to examine government's involvement in producing information about itself. I set out to spend a year observing five press offices (White House, State Department, Pentagon, Food and Drug Administration, and Department of Transportation) from the inside.

Site observation has an honorable tradition in social science research, particularly in cultural anthropology, but I worried that the work of press offices was too politically sensitive to be shared with an outsider. Would the press officers discuss what not to tell reporters while I was looking over their shoulders? What I found was that if I hung around long enough and conducted myself in a nonthreatening manner, they grew used to me and spoke freely in my presence. The research tool was adequate for the task at hand. The result was *The Government/Press Connection*.

Each research design involved learning new tricks of the trade. In the case of site observation, if press officers were to be my South Sea islanders, should I take notes while observing them? No, I decided, unless I was in a meeting where everyone was taking notes. Which meant that I was constantly ducking into the closest men's room to jot down a key quotation or impression.

Unfortunately, site observation did not serve me as well in a subsequent study of congressional reporters. By now I had written two books about Washington journalism. The reporters knew why I was there. (Moreover, I was no longer offering anonymity.) It became clear from some of the exchanges at the press table in the Capitol dining room that some of my South Sea islanders wanted to be memorialized in my next book as latter-day Walter Lippmanns. Clearly there is no technique for all seasons. So I switched to straight interviewing, journalists' own research tool of choice.

Chance too plays a part in any research undertaking. It was merely by chance that I started the press office project in 1981. If the year had been 1984 or even 1983, I probably would have failed. But 1981 was the first year of a new president's term. All presidential administrations initially claim they will be the most open in history, and all draw the wagons more tightly around the White House the longer they are in office. Ronald Reagan's was no exception. But I was able to make my observations at a time when the Reagan appointees still held relatively benign attitudes toward outsiders.

When I moved my research venue to the U.S. Senate in 1984, I decided that the best way to interview legislators was to catch them on the fly. I had seen too many of my colleagues waiting interminably in outer offices for senators who were called away to vote or to greet more important visitors. So each afternoon in the press gallery I would study the next day's schedules to determine where and when the senators I wanted to meet were likely to be, and then I would be there, asking if I might walk along from a committee room back to their office or some such. In the course of the 264 days that the Senate was in session that year I got all the interviews I needed. (I think two senators declined my companionship.) The way I often broke the conversational ice was to say, "Senator, journalists like to place an adjective [like colorful or powerful] in front of a public official's name; if you had your druthers, what adjective would you want to be given?" They seemed to like the game, or at least it stunned them long enough to start an interview. (The adjective they most often chose was hardworking, as in "hardworking Senator John Melcher.")

This study, which became *The Ultimate Insiders* (1986), was focused on which senators get covered by the national media and why. But now, unlike when I studied the Washington press corps, the field was not empty. Research, as a rule, is part of a continuum; the researcher jumps on a moving conveyor belt. On this subject there had been valuable earlier studies by David H. Weaver, G. Cleveland Wilhoit, Joe S. Foote, and others, so that it was possible to show how the national media had increasingly directed attention to the Senate's elected leaders, committee chairmen, and ranking members. This finding seemed to surprise journalists who had been writing that the television age shifted focus to the blow-dried, attention-seeking junior legislators.

In the way research has, interests lead to related interests, one angle leads to another. Congress (to borrow a thought from David Rodgers of the *Wall Street Journal*) turned out to be a big rock candy mountain for researchers. Once I discovered a huge cache of papers in the Senate Radio and Television Gallery that turned out to be a daily record identifying by network or station every TV camera in every Senate committee hearing. Larry Janezich, soon to be director of the gallery, gave me permission to move my corps of intern copyists into the gallery while the reporters were attending the 1984 presidential nominating conventions. Our tabulations demonstrated the extent to which TV favored policy committees (Foreign Relations) over constituency committees (Appropriations). The gallery now publishes these figures monthly.

Similarly, the committees of correspondents who run the congressional press galleries kept minutes of all their meetings, which they were happy to share with me. These records showed under what circumstances the reporters were willing to censure other reporters. Also, since the House and Senate publish salary records of the members' staffs, it was possible to calculate where press secretaries fit in the pecking order. The surprising statistic (given the importance that media are reputed to have on Capitol Hill) is that on average they ranked fifth in the offices of both representatives and senators. The findings appeared in *Live from Capitol Hill!* (1991), the fourth book in the series I called Newswork.

By coming back again and again to the same subjects, albeit from new angles, I was able to measure and comment on change. I watched reporting on Washington matters of regional interest grow in prestige, for instance. In 1978, a third of the reporters on these beats were in their twenties; ten years later, the share had dropped to one-sixth, a sure sign of greater prestige. (There were other signs as well, such as being allowed to do longer stories and travel more.)

These studies often seemed to challenge conventional wisdom. For instance, the importance of local television news to members of Congress is a given in Washington. Yet a survey of fifty-seven stations in thirty-five cities showed how seldom news directors considered the legislators worthy of attention; and, in reviewing 60 hours of local newscasts, I and my assistants saw House members a total of 7 minutes and 45 seconds. Still, I have never set out to be a contrarian. The purpose of research must be simply to test a hypothesis.

The essays in this book, written over a fourteen-year period (1980–94), branch out from the original Newswork research to include thoughts that were first presented in university lectures, magazine articles, and newspaper columns. In the nearly two decades since I stumbled upon Washington journalism as a fitting subject for study, there has been a revolution in scholarly attention focusing on the role of the media in public life. There are now such vibrant centers of enquiry as the Freedom Forum Media Studies Center at Columbia University and the Joan Shorenstein Barone Center on the Press, Politics and Public Policy at Harvard. One scholar claims to have read more than 600 works on political communication published during the 1980s. American government textbooks at the college level in the 1970s often did not even mention the press; today's textbooks devote an entire chapter to the media. When I began this journey in research, I wrote, "Journalists are great fun to study." I have not changed my mind.

For Heidi & Betsy

An Outline of the U.S. News Business

For nearly two years, starting in 1987 in Moscow, citizens of nine cities of the Soviet Union stood in line, often for three or four hours, to see an exhibition called Information USA. On entering, each was given a catalog printed on very durable paper because copies would be read by eight or nine people. I wrote the section on the news media, which follows with updated information. My readers were then living in a closed society, and their views of the United States were limited and undoubtedly distorted. The assignment given to me by the U.S. Information Agency, the exhibition's sponsor, was to "begin at the beginning: provide the historical perspective for how the news media evolved in this country, then move to a discussion of the role that the press plays today." In 3,000 words.

Two blocks from the office building in which I work is a drugstore where I sometimes go to buy small items like toothpaste and film. Near the checkout counter there are racks containing the popular, big-circulation magazines: *Time, Newsweek, Reader's Digest, TV Guide, People*. But there are also less familiar magazines for sale, covering such subjects as working women, science, health, photography, music, movies, and sports. Those who love cooking (and eating) can buy a magazine called *Gourmet*; for the more specialized taste, there is *Chocolatier*, and if one eats too much chocolate, *Weight*

Watchers. On a normal day, there are 260 different magazines displayed in this typical American store. None of them is owned or operated by the government.

A short distance away in this neighborhood is a more unusual shop called Newsroom that stocks several thousand magazines and newspapers. Customers can peruse rows of magazines about specific American cities (*Los Angeles*) or regions (*Louisiana Life*), business magazines (*Financial World*), home magazines (*Architectural Digest*), computer magazines (*Byte*), or some others that contain sexually explicit material.

The magazines for sale at these two stores reflect the huge diversity of what is produced by one segment of the news and entertainment media. These products are not necessarily defined by serious purpose or educational intent. Magazines are part of the information industry of a capitalist society. These are market-oriented products. The defining question is: are there enough potential readers and advertisers to make a publication profitable for its investors? This is a proposition that is constantly being tested with new publications. Among the latest entrants is a magazine directed at grandparents and another for hospital patients. Some of these incipient ventures will not find an appreciative audience or will be badly managed, and they will fail; others will reward their backers for having properly identified a market and then producing a desirable product.

A third store in the neighborhood, called Common Concerns, is similar to outlets found most often in university communities. Its 314 magazine titles, many espousing liberal or radical political and social causes, have names like *Partisan Review, Journal of African Marxists, Journal of Palestine Studies, Greenpeace, Environmental Action, Science for the People*, and *Feminist Directions*. Common Concerns is by no means typical, but it too is part of a very old American tradition.

The politically oriented products of the American information industry usually do not make a profit. They are sustained by the donations of their adherents. These publications have small circulations, although their readers are not necessarily unimportant. Ronald Reagan, for example, said his favorite magazine was *National Review*, a conservative weekly with only 120,000 subscribers when he was president.

The media in America, therefore, form two strands that have peacefully coexisted since the eighteenth century colonial period: the commercial segment, expected to succeed or fail on the operator's ability to make a profit, and offering tremendous diversity to the buying public, and a much smaller but significant noncommercial segment in which almost every interest or shade of opinion is represented by its own publication. More than 11,000 periodicals are published in the United States.

Magazines are just one part of the mix that constitutes the mass media. In broadcasting, too, the choices have proliferated with the increase in radio and television stations and channels. Virtually every home in the United States has at least one television set: out of 96.4 million households, 95.4 million have TVs. Across the country there are 1,137 commercial TV stations and 349 noncommercial stations (often affiliated with universities). Moreover, 62 percent of American homes subscribe to cable TV, and the typical cable system offers thirty to fifty channels.

Ninety-nine percent of all American homes have radios; the average per household is 5.6 (including radios in automobiles). Americans can listen to more than 9,700 radio stations. Most stations are locally owned and controlled and determine their programming independently. Some specialize in popular or classical music; others broadcast news, weather, and sports twenty-four hours a day.

These figures are important not only to show the extent of media saturation, but because polling data suggest that Americans get most of their news from television. Each weeknight, 30 million viewers watch one of three commercial networks' news programs. (Others watch news programs broadcast by the noncommercial Public Broadcasting Service, which is supported by a mix of government and private donations, or the Cable News Network, which broadcasts news and features twenty-four hours a day.)

At the same time, voters—the most politically aware part of the population—are more likely to be newspaper readers. About 1,600 newspapers with a combined circulation of 60 million publish daily in the United States, as well as 7,400 weekly newspapers whose total circulation is 57 million.

One way of understanding the U.S. news media is to examine the evolution of American journalism in terms of the types of individuals who owned the presses.

The Printer (Eighteenth Century)

The first American newspapers were produced by printers, small business owners who used their presses to put out a commercial product in which the news consisted largely of reports on ship arrivals and goods for sale in local stores. According to historian Thomas C. Leonard,

> A colonial print shop was often one press in a single room. . . . It took sixteen hours to set the type for two pages of a newspaper. Two artisans working smoothly together . . . were expected to print 249 sheets an hour. Each page must dry before the process could begin again to print the other side. Through most of the eighteenth century, the four-page weekly paper was not far from the limits of the resources at hand. . . . There was almost no change in the technology of printing in the eighteenth century.

The capabilities of technology would be an important factor in defining the scope of the media throughout this history.

In 1721 in Boston (population 11,000), printer James Franklin (Benjamin Franklin's uncle) added the second strand to American journalism. In addition to commercialism—the wish to profit from his labors—Franklin chose to get into a heated public argument with the authorities. This was in the midst of a smallpox epidemic, and Franklin's *Courant* came out foursquare against inoculation. (Being misguided and stubborn thus has a long tradition in the American press.) From this point forward, according to Leonard, printers "idealized a role of scourge to their community." Skepticism toward authority increasingly became a hallmark of journalism in a democratic society, with part of the journalist's job description being that of extralegal investigator of wrongdoing. (Indeed, today there is an organization called Investigative Reporters and Editors, with a membership of 4,000, whose prime targets are government officials.)

The Partisan (1790s–1830s)

George Washington was unanimously elected the first president of the United States in 1789, but was able to maintain a political consensus for only a short time. His followers divided into two factions, the Federalists of Alexander Hamilton and Thomas Jefferson's Republicans. The opposing factions then created and subsidized newspapers to articulate their points of view.

When the new government established its capital in New York, Hamilton started a Federalist paper there, choosing for its editor John Fenno, who, according to political scientist Richard L. Rubin, was "a polemicist rather than a printer." What Hamilton needed was a fiery writer, not an artisan. Jefferson also chose a political writer, Philip Freneau, to be editor of the Republican paper. Hamilton, as secretary of the treasury, helped to support Fenno with government printing orders; Jefferson, as secretary of state, hired Freneau as a translator in his department, "a position that required little work." However, when Jefferson resigned from government in 1793, Freneau lost his job and his paper soon closed.

Partisan newspapers, which appeared in nearly every city of the young republic, are now remembered more for colorful invective than for newsgathering. These papers, however, did help create the political party system that still defines the politics of the United States. Nevertheless, the lesson for the modern press is that being beholden to politicians and officeholders is a precarious way to run a business.

The Publisher (1830s–1900s)

A new type of newspaper was founded in 1833. The *New York Sun* sold for a penny, one-sixth the price of other newspapers, and within three years it was printing 15,000 copies a day (in 1833 the combined circulation of the city's eleven dailies had been only

26,500). The idea behind the penny press was to seek a large readership that in turn would attract advertisers; the newspapers would be politically independent and would produce timely news aimed at the growing middle class. No longer were the mainstream media to be merely an adjunct of the printer or a vehicle of the politician; they would now be a self-contained branch of commerce under the direction of the publisher.

"The modern mass circulation newspaper would be unimaginable without the technical developments of the early nineteenth century," according to sociologist Michael Schudson, although while technology "made mass circulation newspapers possible, it did not make them necessary or inevitable." The steam press replaced the hand press; the cylinder press replaced the flatbed; paper, which had formerly been made mostly from rags, could now be produced from inexpensive ground wood pulp because of a process invented in 1844. The development of lithography meant that drawings could be reproduced at a much lower cost. The railroads brought lumber to the mills and paper to the printing plants. The telegraph came into use in the 1840s, and its wires brought news of war with Mexico to American readers in 1846. News could be more current. Newspapers could be printed fast and cheaply.

The second half of the nineteenth century also saw the rise of the great press lords, such as Joseph Pulitzer and William Randolph Hearst, whose battles to increase circulation, especially those between Hearst's *Journal* and Pulitzer's *World* in New York, featured glaring headlines, color comics, numerous illustrations, and sensational articles, the most sensational of which helped plunge the United States into war with Spain in 1898.

The Corporation (Twentieth Century)

In 1848 a group of New York newspapers organized the first wire service or news agency, the Associated Press. The purpose of the cooperative was to use the same reporters to gather news for all the member publications. According to journalism educator Fred S. Siebert, "the news agencies instructed reporters and writers to remember that their writings were being distributed to both Democratic and Republican newspapers and other clients, and had to be acceptable to both. Writers became adept at constructing nonpartisan accounts, and from this practice grew the concept of objective reporting which has permeated American journalism to the present."

If objective reporting was rooted in technology (the development of telegraphy) and economics (the profit in expanding diverse audiences), it was advanced by the desire to turn journalism into a profession. (The first training school for journalists was created at the University of Missouri in 1908.) As a reaction to the sensationalism of the press lords' era, objective reporting was meant to separate fact from opinion, try to keep reporters' personal views out of their writing, and at the same time tell more than one side of a story. If a reporter's opinion was stated, the article was expected to be labeled as opinion or placed in the editorial section of the newspaper. The coming of the wire services vastly expanded the quantity of news available to individual papers, but also added to the sameness of the product. As he crossed the country in 1930, Oswald Garrison Villard, editor of the *Nation*, noted that the same stories appeared in the papers he bought at each train stop.

As technology widened the reach of communications, increased the costs of acquiring or starting media enterprises, and expanded the potential profits, the news business in the twentieth century followed some of the same tendencies toward greater consolidation that can be seen in other major industries, such as automobiles and oil. In 1900 the 8 largest newspaper companies controlled perhaps 10 percent of the national daily circulation; today more than 70 percent of U.S. daily newspapers are owned by business groups, and the 20 largest companies in this business own a total of 502 newspapers.

Some media critics such as Ben H. Bagdikian find fault with this trend because they claim it puts too much power into too few hands: "No small group, certainly no group with as much uniformity of outlook as large corporations, can be sufficiently open and flexible to reflect the fullness of society's values and wishes." Others contend that large media companies no longer need be influenced by the politics of their advertisers; smaller operators might not have been able to afford this independence.

The same centralizing impetus can be seen in the television business. Although federal government regulations do not permit one company to own more than twelve TV stations, most stations are joined contractually to one of four competing national networks (ABC, CBS, NBC, Fox), which provide them with much of their programming. This means that Americans, regardless of where they live, see the same news broadcasts at breakfast and dinner, although noncommercial public broadcasting, other independent stations, and the proliferation of cable TV are diversifying the outlets for televised news and information.

What is the future in an industry experiencing such rapid technological change? Gary Orren of Harvard University predicts that despite the current centralization of the media, advanced technology is likely to produce greater decentralization. One key to decentralization is the satellite. In the Washington press corps, for instance, the greatest growth since 1979 has been among TV reporters representing stations from every part of the United States. Satellite transmission allows them to beam material from Washington that is of special local interest without relying on the commercial networks. The stories arrive at their home stations almost instantly.

According to Orren, whatever the mix of media, there will be more of it. Printed matter did not disappear when radio appeared, and radio did not disappear when television appeared. In the same vein, we can expect to have newspapers, magazines, radio, and television coexisting with newer forms of communicating such as computer-to-computer electronic mail, or teletext, which delivers textual and graphic information to TV screens. In short, the new media will supplement, not replace, the diversity of news media that now exists.

The Media and Government

How much do the news media affect political and governmental actions? The press influences public opinion and public opinion influences government officials. The problem for researchers is that it is difficult to show cause and effect except in the most dramatic cases. It is well known, for example, that the investigating of *Washington Post* reporters Carl Bernstein and Bob Woodward helped to expose the Watergate scandals that led to the resignation of President

Richard Nixon in 1974. Since most campaigning for high office is now done via television, we also assume that there is an electoral connection, that candidates who make the best impressions on TV have the best chance of winning. Yet as Herbert J. Gans of Columbia University has noted, "After more than twenty-five years of television news, the country has still elected only two telegenic presidents, John F. Kennedy and Ronald Reagan." Gans contends that television has much greater impact on political communication (what government officials say) than it does on political action (what the public or officials do); thus the main consequence of TV on American politics is stylistic.

But Lloyd N. Cutler, an adviser to Presidents Jimmy Carter and Bill Clinton, has argued that White House officials believe it is obligatory for them to respond to network news stories (presumably to see that the facts are right or to put their own spin on them) and that this speeds up decisionmaking. "In a very real sense," he has commented, "TV lead stories now set the priorities for the policymaking agenda."

Others believe, as Bernard C. Cohen wrote in 1963, the press "may not be successful much of the time in telling readers what to think, but it is stunningly successful in telling readers what to think *about*." In other words, the most significant function of the press is to serve as gatekeeper, choosing for readers and listeners what issues and persons are most important from among the many subjects vying for public attention.

The news media may not be a fourth branch of government, as they have been called. Still, they are more than passive observers. Events happen differently because media are observing them. Officials must ask themselves, "How would this look on TV or the front page?" Some ideas are moved to greater prominence because of decisions by journalists. Some voters decide whether to retain or remove their elected representatives on the basis of information that comes from newspapers, magazines, radio, and television. Journalism's impact has become much greater since it moved out of the printer's shop.

The Washington Reporter as Insider

James Q. Wilson, the political scientist, once noted that organizations come to resemble the organizations they are in conflict with. Daniel Patrick Moynihan then applied this observation to government in Washington, calling his theory the Iron Law of Emulation. The burgeoning bureaucracy of the legislature, for example, has begun to look like the burgeoned bureaucracy of the executive branch. It is as if a football team had adopted the formations of the opposition. Much of this sort of analogy also applies to the interface of news media and government: two institutions in conflict increasingly resembling each other.

The most obvious resemblance is in personnel. The denizens of government's executive suites and those of the Washington bureaus of the major news organizations are becoming interchangeable. In socioeconomic terms—schools attended, income, spouses' backgrounds, the neighborhoods they live in—they increasingly look alike; in personal terms, some *are* the same people. At least eleven journalists have served in both the *New York Times* Washington bureau and in some recent presidential administration. The most fascinating and commented upon case is the Gelb–Burt exchange.

From a paper delivered at the symposium "Informing America: Who is Responsible for What?" Syracuse University, April 23, 1985; also *Communication*, vol. 8, no. 2 (1985).

Leslie Gelb left the *Times* at the beginning of the Carter administration in 1977 to become director of politico-military affairs at the Department of State, staying into 1979. Richard Burt left the Washington bureau of the *Times* for the same job at the beginning of the Reagan presidency in 1981; Gelb returned to the *Times* in 1981 as its national security correspondent. Although reporters once took jobs in government primarily as press secretaries or speechwriters, the Gelb and Burt examples show that they are now moving into policy positions. Another index of this phenomenon is the membership roster of the prestigious Council on Foreign Relations, which lists at least 130 persons who are or have been journalists, nearly 40 of whom are Washington practitioners.

Rhetorical allusions to big government and big media do not fit the Washington I am describing. The upper echelon of the State Department, including people with titles such as Assistant Legal Adviser for Special Functional Problems, is about the size of a large Houston law firm. The odds that a diplomatic correspondent of long standing knows one of these people by first name is only a little better than the odds that a partner in Vinson & Elkins knows the first name of a randomly selected member of his firm. But this Washington is growing larger: in 1943 there were four assistant secretaries of state; now there are fourteen. In 1943 there were three reporters in the *Los Angeles Times* bureau; now there are twenty-five. Still, it is a small world.

The coming together of national journalists and those they report about is the by-product of a forced march to professionalism and specialization in both endeavors. Public administration and journalism have been occupations in search of professional standing since the turn of the century. Woodrow Wilson wrote that there should be a science of government administration, and universities have been attempting to realize that vision ever since. Journalists, in their quest for self-improvement and acceptability, created training schools (University of Missouri, 1908), honorary societies (Sigma Delta Chi, 1910), awards for excellence (Pulitzer prizes, 1917), professional organizations (American Society of Newspaper Editors, 1922), codes of ethics, professional journals (*Columbia Journalism Review*, 1961), and, at the pinnacle of respectability, Ph.D. programs in mass communications (University of Minnesota, 1950).

By the time the Washington government was ready to burst into a New Deal, journalism, too, had an embryonic professional infrastructure in place. In 1935, the middle of the Great Depression, Leo Rosten, a graduate student at the University of Chicago, came to Washington to survey the press corps. He discovered that 51 percent of the reporters had college degrees and another 28 percent had some college training. Haynes Johnson, of the *Washington Post*, has said that in the 1930s his father, a Pulitzer-prize-winning reporter, used to lecture on "the myth of *The Front Page*," challenging the stereotype of the lower class, ill-educated journalist depicted in the popular Ben Hecht–Charles MacArthur play.

The best predictor of emerging professional status is educational attainment. By 1978, almost every Washington reporter had been to college, almost half had gone to graduate school, a third had advanced degrees, and 6 percent had earned law degrees or doctorates. Washington reporters also attended very good schools. By comparing their alma maters with ratings in a standard college guide, it was possible to conclude that 35 percent of the national press corps attended highly selective schools: the Ivy League and such other institutions as Amherst, Brandeis, Bryn Mawr, Carleton, University of Chicago, Haverford, Johns Hopkins, MIT, Mount Holyoke, Oberlin, Reed, Rice, Smith, Stanford, Swarthmore, Wellesley, and Williams. This is especially true of those on such news beats as diplomacy, politics, and economics.

Forty percent of Washington reporters consider themselves specialists. The definition of specialization in journalism is, however, somewhat looser than in other professions: a tax lawyer would not consider an experienced reporter covering the IRS (perhaps with an M.A. in economics) to be a specialist. Still, 40 percent is a remarkable statistic. Historically, journalism had been the last refuge of the generalist.

As Washington bureaus get larger, specialization flourishes. Reporters in a bureau of three or fewer are generalists; in a six-person bureau, two reporters are specialists; in a ten-person bureau, four are specialists. When a bureau has twenty reporters, only five or six are on general assignments. The trend in Washington journalism is also in the direction of specialized publications in which specialist journalists report on the work of government specialists. The publications represented in the Congressional Periodicals Gallery range from *Air Quality Week* to *Waterways Journal.*

Advances in professionalism and specialization are expensive for bosses and workers. The prospective employee is required to buy more education. The employer pays a premium for that education. Generalist journalists are fungible: when there is no fire, they can be sent to cover a robbery. But what to do with a specialist on the Supreme Court beat, most likely with a law degree, when the Court is in recess? Moreover, specialists demand more autonomy, which means that control of the final product may gradually drift from the news processors (editors) to the newsgatherers (reporters). Specialists are also more satisfied with their work, which means that they may stay in journalism longer, and, of course, stay longer on the same beat. This could make the news business somewhat less lucrative for media owners because personnel costs rise with seniority. As the specialists remain in place there will be less room for the entering journalist. The journalism business has traditionally thrived on an unstable personnel system—reporters drifting into other lines of work keep costs down and make room for younger aspirants.

A drawback of increased specialization in any profession is that it carries with it its own language. Yale University Press published a book in 1984 in which David M. Ricci, a political scientist, accused his academic brethren of holding small conversations. "Small conversations take place in many learned disciplines, when members of a scholarly community speak mainly to one another, in language so specialized and full of jargon that it is largely unintelligible to the public." Given the purpose of the mass media, a press corps of jargonauts would be a disaster. In early June 1982, when President Reagan went to Europe to attend an economic summit conference at Versailles, he was escorted by a Boeing 747 filled with White House, diplomatic, and economics reporters. "The blending of these three press corps was fascinating," Lou Cannon of the *Washington Post* told me. "Each asked questions in its own jargon. For example, questions about 'confidence-building mechanisms' always came from State Department reporters."

Although reporters have to guard against these tendencies, jargon need not be a major concern in the popular press as long as generalist editors are doing their jobs. The problem will arise if editors are intimidated by their specialists. And this is possible. A survey I have conducted suggests that generalist reporters have more disagreements with their home offices than do specialists, including disputes over story length and writing style. In the newsroom of the *Baltimore Sun*, one of the editors told me that their Pentagon correspondent is called "The General." Who argues with a general?

As the Washington journalist and the government source increasingly look like the same person performing different tasks, more stories will slip into print that are fascinating to those involved but irrelevant or uninteresting to those who make their living in other ways.

On December 19 and December 21, 1984, front-page articles in the *New York Times* detailed what became known in Washington as the Shultz Shuffle or the Shultz Purge (depending on one's point of view). Taken together, the two articles listed ten job changes that Secretary of State George Shultz was expected to make, five at the assistant secretary level and five ambassadorial posts in Latin America. Most of the predicted changes were to be replacements of conservative political appointees with Foreign Service officers.

One White House adviser said, "the Shultz people got the jump on the conservatives by moving swiftly, quietly and with some stealth on these appointments. The conservatives didn't know what was happening until it was pretty well set. Now they're trying to respond." (One characteristic of the insider story is that quotations are mostly attributed to "a ranking administration official," a "senior administration official," or just "officials." Usually this is a disservice to readers, who have no way of knowing what axes the anonymous speakers are grinding.)

Edwin J. Feulner, Jr., president of the conservative Heritage Foundation, was quoted as saying, "this is the first roundup leading to a Christmas massacre." "It's no such thing," replied the *New York Times* lead editorial of December 22. "There is an ominous overtone in the agitated needling of Mr. Shultz." Columnists joined in with their own interpretations. Rowland Evans and Robert Novak viewed the proposed changes as meaning that "Shultz [is] now in the close embrace of the Foreign Service." Suzanne Garment thought otherwise. Shultz, "the wily secretary," was merely buying off the careerists, and at a good price.

Whether the *Times* articles proved to be essentially correct is not the point I am raising. Some of the personnel changes were made, some were not. The reporter apparently had good sources, and, as the saying goes, a daily newspaper is only the first draft of history. What should have been clear, however, without having to rely on hindsight is that the jobs in dispute had longer titles than they had power. They were distinctly middle-level positions. For conservatives to fight over any potential losses, no matter how slight, is appropriate. For the *Times* to devote two front-page stories to such squabbles is to assume that the outcomes would be of interest to the majority of its subscribers or that the outcomes were important in their effects on U.S. foreign policy.

Times columnist James Reston would later list such personnel tales as "among the many puzzling pleasures and trivial pursuits" of Washington. Capital residents divide the world between inside and outside the beltway: these were inside-the-beltway stories.

An ombudsman of the *Washington Post*, Sam Zagoria, reminded readers in January 1985 that his paper had published twelve series between Thanksgiving and New Year's week, amounting to more than 5,000 inches of type, covering such subjects as "Africa: The Hungry Continent," "Whoops" (the Washington Public Power Supply System), "Inside the Geographic" (the *National Geographic* magazine), "Fundamentalism: The New Old-Time Religion," Nicaragua's "Secret War," "Lean, Green and Mean: The Army of the 80s," "Riding the Red Line: Four More Stations" (about Washington's subway), and "The Roots of Biotechnology." Zagoria made it clear that he believed the *Post* was guilty of journalistic overkill. "How many of you," he asked, "read even one complete segment of any one of the series from beginning to end?" He said he received calls in support of his position. Editor Leonard Downie was not dismayed by the lengthy pieces. "I don't really expect a series to be read word for word," he said. "They serve different publics." (They also win prizes for newspapers.)

One of the most often heard complaints about generalist journalism is that it does not treat issues with sufficient depth. Business executives testify that coverage of their concerns is shallow, as do those involved in public health, education, international relations, and so forth. But the debate between Zagoria and Downie is really about the coming of specialist journalism, whose hallmark will be a great deal of in-depth coverage on topics that interest the specialists. Assuming that the newshole is finite (if something goes into a newspaper or broadcast, something else will have to come out), care will have to be taken to balance the interests of the specialists who are the writers and the generalists who make up most of the audience.

The case that can be made against the way the *Post* covered the 1984 race for the Democratic presidential nomination includes overkill and insideritis. Again, the criticism is not one of insufficient resources—five national reporters, the political editor, and a researcher were in New Hampshire on its primary night—nor of the skill of the staff, perhaps the best group of political reporters in the country.

On March 4, 1984, the *Post* ran twelve election stories or opinion columns, by twelve reporters or columnists, amounting to more than 12,000 words; on March 25 the totals were fourteen stories or columns, by fourteen reporters or columnists, adding up to 11,000 words. Reading again the campaign coverage, one is reintroduced to a cast of characters quoted or referred to: Robert Beckel, Kathy Bushkin, Patrick Caddell, Charles Campion, Tim Hagen, William Hamilton, Oliver (Pudge) Henkel, James Johnson, Robert J. Keefe, Richard Moe, Jeanne Shaheen, Paul Shone, Robert D. Squier, Gerald T. Vento. If you cannot identify half of these players, then the game—as reported—is not your favorite sport.

Richard E. Neustadt, I believe, was the first to write about "inners and outers," a select few who always seem to show up in high appointed office when their party captures the White House and who then return to careers in such professions as law, banking, and academia until the next opportunity for public service. The academy generally honors its inner-outers for bringing a sense of realism to the teaching of international relations and political science.

Only in recent years have the inner-outers included journalists. There always have been former journalists in government, but rarely did they return to the news business. The distinction of being first to go from journalism to government to journalism to government to journalism—the true test of the inner-outer—may belong to Eileen Shanahan, whose resume reads: *Journal of Commerce*, Treasury Department during the Kennedy administration, *New York Times*, Department of Health, Education and Welfare during the Carter administration, *Washington Star*.

Journalism—unlike academe—still is not sure how to deal with its inner-outers. On the one hand, their experiences in government usually add richness to their reportage. On the other hand, how sure can news organizations be that these reporters do not have hidden agendas, lists of policies that they mean to promote or work against?

Inner-outer Leslie Gelb argues that news organizations should be wary of hiring reporters who have held policy or advocacy positions in government. There is no problem, however, with former government officials such as columnists George Will, William Safire, and Carl Rowan whose writings are clearly labeled as opinion. Still, there should be some way to make exceptions in unusual cases, some litmus test that can measure the intensity of one's ideology or the strength of one's convictions. Shanahan has contended that reentry into journalism must be based only on a boss's evaluation of the official's past record in the news business, particularly on his or her commitment to the rules of balance and fairness that govern mainstream journalism.

There is, in observing presidential politics, a sort of bend-over-backwards factor: that which we worry most about in a candidate is often that which we have least need to worry about in a president. When former General Dwight Eisenhower, for instance, left the White House, he warned against the military-industrial complex. If there is a bend-over-backwards factor in the emerging journalism of Washington, it is in reaction to the fear that the specialist journalist will be coopted by the specialist official, who could be beholden to sources and functioning as a cheerleader for an agency or a policy. More worrisome than developing an enthusiasm for the agency covered is the possibility that the beat reporter will become less understanding of the viewpoints of the agency's critics.

Herbert J. Gans, who is a careful observer of the news media, contends that "surrendering to temptation may give reporters short-run advantages over their colleagues, but it is fatal in the long run, for once reporters have developed a reputation of having been co-opted, they lose the confidence of their peers and superiors." The high regard of one's colleagues is particularly important in the

Washington press corps, where nearly half of reporters' closest friends are also in journalism. (The comparable figure for journalists throughout the United States is less than a third.)

So far the specialist in journalism is first a journalist, then a specialist. Most of those with law degrees, for example, attended law school after they had worked for a news organization. Frederick Taylor, explaining the practice of the *Wall Street Journal*, told me, "It's easier to make a reporter into an economist than an economist into a reporter." When the profession of journalism and the profession of the reporter's beat clash, journalism, with its emphasis on controversy, will always win. The contest resembles the children's game of paper covers rock.

As the Iron Law of Emulation takes hold in Washington's government-press relations, there will be one surprising development: the Hess corollary to the Moynihan law. As organizations in conflict increasingly resemble each other, they will fight more, and over less.

The steadily rising number of public brouhahas between the Washington press corps and the Reagan administration has been blamed by the press on the hostility of the Reaganites and by the Reaganites on the reporters' ideology or questionable patriotism. In fact, the Reagan administration falls in the middle on any realistic scale of presidential hostility toward the media since 1945, and the media's treatment of this presidency also is in the middle range, possibly half way between the treatment of Kennedy and Nixon. There have been more fights, yet, with the exception of excluding reporters from Grenada, it is difficult to recall what the skirmishes were about.

Each day there will be some information that a reporter wants and that a government official does not want to give. Journalists are justly proud of the fights they wage over freedom of information. There are government officials who defend their responsibility for protecting national security with equal righteousness. Government-press battles loom very large from up close. But if we step back a moment, what comes into focus is that the battles are being fought within relatively narrow parameters. Partly this is because government is good at protecting its real secrets, partly because no serious news organization would publish material that it feels might endanger the nation. But mainly, given the Iron Law of Emulation, the reason is that officials and journalists now hold very similar views of society and similar views of government's role. Reporters and their sources are closer in outlook to each other than to the rest of the populace.

The city of Washington was created solely for the purpose of being the seat of government. The absence of commerce and industry, as well as other nongovernmental pursuits, helps give a hermetically sealed quality to concerns in the capital. Perhaps the Founding Fathers made a mistake in not locating the federal government in a place where attention would have to be shared with other interests.

Washington insiders are different. There is a self-selection process in any calling. No one is forced to work as a government insider. The fact that government workers and newspeople choose to live in Washington implies that they are uniquely interested in politics, diplomacy, and public policy. But those who choose not to come to Washington, I think, are increasingly finding government of minor interest at best, and, more often, a major irritant in their lives. The best that Washington journalists can do is to accurately explain this world of insiders to others.

All the Presidents' Reporters

n July and August 1991, thirteen years after having first surveyed the White House press corps, I retraced my steps to find out what had happened to the president's reporters. Who are these journalists? Are they different from their colleagues? What, especially, do they do? Does it make any difference who covers the president?

Mark J. Rozell, writing in *The Press and the Carter Presidency*, has claimed they "teach the public about what presidents should and should not be doing, how presidents should lead, and whether presidents are succeeding or failing the task of leadership." Mark Hertsgaard, observing the White House reporters during the Reagan presidency, has warned, "The value judgments American journalists make in reporting the news are inevitably influenced by their own backgrounds." While historian Henry Graff, taking a more visionary position, has characterized the media's role in creating the presidential persona as "the ether, the invisible avenue through which we are led and by which our governance is conducted." (I shall return to the question of whether who covers the president makes any difference.)

Although there are some 2,000 journalists accredited to cover the White House, the White House press corps is the name given to

From a lecture in the series, The Future of Presidential Power, University of Wisconsin, November 7, 1991; also *Presidential Studies Quarterly*, vol. 22 (Spring 1992).

about 60 reporters, the regulars, who have assigned seats at the press secretary's daily briefings, a desk in the pressroom, and who usually travel with the president. My 1991 survey interviewed 39 of these regulars. The group included representatives from the wire services (AP, UPI, Reuters), each of which maintains up to 4 reporters at the White House; the TV networks (ABC, CBS, NBC, CNN), also with staffs of 3 or 4; some major newspapers (*New York Times, Washington Post, Wall Street Journal, Los Angeles Times*) and the weekly newsmagazines with 2 reporters; and smaller newspapers, magazines, and newspaper chains that cover the White House with one full-time reporter.

These reporters represent mainstream organizations, and as such they follow the rules of their craft that determine what is news, length of story, standards of objectivity, rules of civility (as defined by libel law and their consumers), and appropriate conventions of sourcing. They are not advocates. They are not literati.

Given the high cost of maintaining journalists at the White House and the continuing news industry consolidation, the president's reporters generally work for large organizations. This means that they are experienced, older journalists. Covering the president is not an entry-level job. These reporters started their careers years ago someplace else, eventually moved to Washington, and were finally elevated to the White House beat.

They are journalists who report on the activities of one person. With the exception of a few magazine writers, notably at the *National Journal* and the *New Republic*, they do not concern themselves with institutional matters. They cover the president, not the presidency.

The prestige of the beat comes from constant exposure, the reporter's byline on page one or his or her face on the network news, rather than from the opportunity for creativity or even enjoyment. White House reporters are important because the person they report on is important. This exposure is particularly valuable for television correspondents: Dan Rather, Tom Brokaw, Sam Donaldson, and Leslie Stahl all moved up to their present perches from the White House pressroom. An advantage for print reporters is the possibility of lucrative freelance assignments. (Nearly half the reporters surveyed were engaged in writing books, magazine articles, or some other extra activity.

Following a president involves a great deal of travel. Don Campbell, a former White House reporter for the Gannett News Service,
described it this way: "Life on the beat approximates being one of
the four-legged members of the support cast in an old western movie
about cattle drives. On the road, you are constantly being herded
from photo opportunity to press plane to motorcade bus to background briefing to hotel pressroom." Yet despite complaints, when
measuring the prestige of Washington assignments, the more exotic
the travel, the more attractive the beat. Katmandu outshines Peoria
and Timbuktu beats Ashtabula.

Here are the basic facts of the 1991 White House press corps: it is
69 percent male, 31 percent female, 95 percent white, 5 percent
minorities. These figures are close to the percentages for all journalists in the nation and represent substantial gains in Washington,
where in 1978 the hiring of female reporters lagged behind the rest
of the United States by seven years. Yet if Washington journalism
has caught up with journalism nationally, the news business generally
still lags behind other industries, where women make up 44 percent
of the professional workforce and minorities account for 10 percent.

In several other respects the composition of the White House
press corps has become more like the nation at large. After my 1978
survey, I wrote, "If there is an average Washington reporter and an
average American, they do not look much like each other." But
now reporters and other Americans are coming together in the
percentages from urban and rural backgrounds and from the different
regions of the country, although midwesterners are overrepresented
among journalists and westerners are underrepresented. The White
House reporters, however, are not nearly as close to being typical
Americans as are the reporters who cover Congress. While 16 percent of the congressional reporters are in their twenties, for example,
no White House reporter in our sample was younger than thirty-two.

The mean age for journalists at the White House is forty-two.
They have been journalists on average for nineteen years, and
Washington reporters for thirteen years. This is an older and more
experienced group than the one in 1978, when they averaged
thirty-nine years of age, with seven years as a journalist before
coming to Washington and seven years in Washington. These differ-

ences have more to do with the election of Jimmy Carter than with a deliberate decision on the part of news organizations to put more seasoned reporters on the beat.

Many news operations, particularly the television networks, give the White House assignment to the reporter who has covered the winning presidential candidate, the logic being that he or she will have developed contacts and insights while on the campaign trail. (It also means that the reporter has a vested interest in a candidate.) During George Bush's administration, for instance, about one-fifth of the White House press had covered his 1988 campaign. But in 1976 the campaign of a former Georgia governor for the Democratic nomination was initially given low priority and assigned to more junior reporters. Veterans were following such luminaries as Birch Bayh, Frank Church, and Henry Jackson. "Jimmy Who" surprised the news executives, and after his inauguration, as one example, Judy Woodruff, who had been an Atlanta-based general assignments reporter only a few months before, became NBC's White House correspondent. She was thirty years old.

Changing presidential reporters when presidents change precipitates a round of musical chairs among Washington journalists. A new White House correspondent means that a place must be found for the old White House correspondent. Send him to the State Department and a place must be found for the old State Department correspondent, and so forth. This excuse for rotation generally has a salutary effect on news organizations. But it also ensures that the White House press corps will be short on historical memory. Of those in my 1991 survey, 51 percent had covered only George Bush, another 36 percent had covered Ronald Reagan and Bush. Fewer than a half dozen were in the White House during the administrations of three or more presidents.

There is virtually no difference in age or overall experience between the men and women on the beat, although women on average have been at the White House a year longer. The reporters tend to have been sent there in their mid- to late thirties. A mean age of forty-two is about right for covering a president. It is a time when the energy line crosses the wisdom line, energy and wisdom being useful commodities in this assignment. As reporters grow older, they may have more wisdom and less energy.

It is remarkable how few differences there are between male and female reporters at the White House. They have gone to public and private colleges in the same proportion, majored in the same subjects, have been as likely to attend graduate school, have read the same publications, watched the same TV shows, done the same amount of freelance work, and argued with their editors over the same matters. Women are, however, more satisfied in their work, more centrist in their politics, and less likely to number other journalists among their closest friends.

Many reporters come from the upper middle class. Although 80 percent of Americans go to public colleges and universities, 53 percent of the reporters attended private schools. They are nearly all college graduates (95 percent); half have had some postgraduate schooling and a third have earned graduate degrees. The sample turned up three reporters with law degrees. Rated on a common selectivity scale, half went to good universities and another fourth went to prestigious ones such as Harvard, MIT, and Cornell.

These reporters defy a strong trend toward majoring in journalism. More than 80 percent of the entry-level applicants for journalism jobs are journalism majors. This trend is clear in my survey of reporters covering Congress, where journalism graduates increased from 36 to 49 percent in the decade between 1978 and 1988. But at the White House the percentage of journalism majors has dropped from 41 percent in 1978 to 37 percent in 1991, while the proportion of humanities and liberal arts majors increased from 52 to 58 percent. The same pattern—both over time and in comparing the White House and Congress beats—holds for graduate studies.

Because White House reporters tend to be older, and because other data show that the older the reporter the less likely he or she is to have majored in journalism, an easy explanation is that this phenomenon is merely a product of age. But as Richard Nixon might have said, "this would be wrong." The reporters at the White House who majored in journalism are no younger on average than those who did not. A modest percentage point or two, not more, might be attributed to the larger number of White House reporters who attended elite schools that do not have journalism departments. Otherwise, this is a puzzlement.

Congressional reporters in television are more likely to be journalism majors. Again, this is not true of the White House press corps: the journalism majors covering the president most often work for important newspapers. Ann Devroy of the *Washington Post*, for instance, was a journalism major at the University of Wisconsin. Other than journalism, the undergraduate majors of choice are English literature, political science, and history, in that order. White House reporters, then and now, are woefully uninterested in economics and the natural sciences.

When surveying Capitol Hill journalists in 1988, I found that television and print reporters had distinct profiles. They did not look much like each other. The so-called pretty-face syndrome was evident among TV journalists, who were more apt to be young and female and working for local stations. But the television people at the White House work for the networks and, although it is harder to generalize because the numbers are small, no significant differences seem to exist between the media. Television and print reporters, for example, have equal levels of formal education. They even argue with their editors or producers about the same thing: the length of their stories. Print reporters, however, have gone to more prestigious schools, done more freelance work, and are more likely to have other journalists as their closest friends.

The reporters were asked a series of questions about their reading and viewing habits and, as expected, they are news junkies who consume four or five daily newspapers. They all read the *Washington Post*, thirty-eight of thirty-nine read the *New York Times*, and then, in descending order, the *Wall Street Journal* (85 percent), the *Washington Times* (51 percent), *USA Today* (31 percent), and the *Los Angeles Times* (18 percent). There was one reader of the *Racing Form*.

The reporters read an average of five different magazines, with one reporter claiming to be a regular reader of fourteen. Ninety percent read at least one weekly newsmagazine: *Newsweek* had an 85 percent readership, *Time* 77 percent, *U.S. News & World Report* 56 percent. Otherwise, the magazines of choice are the *New Republic*, 59 percent, the *Economist*, 28 percent, the *New Yorker*, 21 percent, and *Vanity Fair*, 21 percent. There are many readers of sports and hobbies magazines, but hardly any of journalism reviews, foreign

policy magazines, business weeklies, or ideological journals (either of
the left or the right). Theirs is not a specialist's bibliography. To the
degree that their reading fills a need to know, the tilt is toward those
publications that feature politics–cum–current events.

The television networks' evening news programs are not as
crucial to White House reporters' need to know as in 1978.
Reporters now watch them an average of three nights a week; in
1978 they watched five nights a week. They average three morn-
ings a week, the same as in 1978. The averages, however, are
deceptive because they are made up of twelve reporters who rarely
watch either the morning or evening news, twelve who watch
both, and the high–lows, six of whom watch in the morning but
not the evening and six who watch at night but not in the morning.
These groups do not neatly divide by sex, age, or the type of news
organization they work for, other than that television reporters like
to watch themselves. (Of the two New York Times reporters at the
White House, for instance, one watches television very little and
the other a great deal.)

This decline in watching network news may simply reflect the
increased fractionalizing of television audiences across the country.
The number of network TV viewers decreased about 25 percent in
the period between the two surveys. Yet some White House reporters may also have made a qualitative decision. Twenty of thirty-nine,
or 51 percent, did not watch any of the weekend interview programs. The average for the group was barely one program per
reporter, and it was this high because one reporter claimed to watch
six shows.

Burt Solomon, a magazine reporter who does not get to the
White House every day, said he watches the evening news to remind
himself of the tone of the presidency. But there must be other White
House reporters who listen to these programs out of habit or for
entertainment, not as a source of useful material for their work. Still,
there is another explanation for the drop in television viewing. For
the sake of symmetry, I was probably asking 1978 questions that do
not adequately account for the rise of CNN, which, as a nonstop
conveyer belt of information, is a constant presence in most newsrooms and thus takes the edge off the hard news value of the
network programs.

Much of the media manipulation during the Michael Deaver era at the Reagan White House was directed at network television, the medium through which most Americans learn the news. Yet the 1991 survey suggests that ordinarily (as opposed to times of crises, when everyone, including presidents, turns on the set) it is the print media that circulate information at the elite level, the level of "informed sources."

White House reporters have continued to be a satisfied lot, but not as satisfied as they were in 1978. Then, when asked about job satisfaction, all reporters interviewed claimed to be either very or fairly satisfied. The job satisfaction figure in 1991 dropped to 85 percent. The decline did not relate to circumstances in the White House pressroom. Most reporters were not there when Jody Powell was President Carter's press secretary, and thus could not make comparisons. But the old-timers were not grumbling more than usual. President Bush's spokesman got high marks. As Carl Leubsdorf, of the *Dallas Morning News*, noted, "Marlin Fitzwater doesn't have a mean bone in his body."

The problem was largely dissatisfaction with their own organizations. We asked reporters to rate levels of disagreement with their home offices on nine scales, such as money for travel and expenses; they indicated more conflict in seven of the nine categories. The two areas in which they claimed less disagreement than in 1978 were disputes over story length and time to write. Not that news organizations have turned into snake pits. Reporters were asked to rate areas of friction on a scale of "never-seldom-sometimes-often," and their answers fell between "seldom" and "sometimes." But there may have been another cause for discontent in the White House pressroom: midlife crisis. The 1978 study found a slight drop in job satisfaction when reporters reached their forties. However, they snap back after fifty.

There are some who think that White House reporters are too satisfied. In 1978 when they were asked about "being out of touch with people 'out there'—meaning the rest of the nation"—88 percent said that this was a serious problem; none thought it was not a problem. The resurvey found that the "serious problem" response had dipped to 40 percent and "not a problem" had risen to 18 percent. Half the reporters also thought that pack or herd journalism was also a serious problem at the White House, although this figure was down slightly from 1978.

Especially revealing in defining a world of journalists that is becoming increasingly insular is that most of the friends of White House journalists are other journalists. In responses to the question, "Of your three closest friends in Washington, excluding family, how many are in journalism?" the average was 1.7; about 1.5 for women, 1.9 for men. In other words at the White House, half the women reporters' closest friends were journalists, and two-thirds of the male reporters' closest friends were journalists. This pattern is very different from that for journalists outside Washington, who are more likely to be linked through friendships with the rest of the community.

There is a good deal of evidence, mostly in the form of straw polls, that Washington reporters overwhelmingly vote for the more liberal presidential candidates. In the 1978 survey of all Washington reporters, 42 percent considered themselves liberals, 39 percent said they were middle-of-the-road, and only 19 percent identified themselves as conservatives. While the sample was too small to draw conclusions about the politics of the White House beat, there are reasons to believe that as employees of larger, more influential news organizations these reporters were to the left of their colleagues who worked for smaller or more specialized publications. Thirteen years, and two conservative presidents later, we asked, "On a scale of four with four being very conservative politically and one being very liberal, where would you place yourself?" Of the thirty-three reporters who responded, 42.4 percent considered themselves liberal, 24.2 percent middle of the road, and 33.3 percent conservative. Thus the White House press corps might best be characterized as liberal *and* considerably more conservative than it used to be. According to Julia Malone of Cox Newspapers, "You don't find many New Dealers in this crowd." Even ABC's Brit Hume, an outspoken conservative, claimed to have seen White House reporters sing the national anthem. "That," he said, "is new." Most conservatives are men between the ages of forty and forty-nine; half those in their thirties and fifties are liberal and half conservative; women place themselves in the middle, but they were least likely to answer the question. Television reporters are more conservative than newspaper reporters.

We also asked White House reporters whether they thought they were to the right or the left of "the whole Washington press corps." Of those who answered, 48 percent said they were to the right, 30 percent judged themselves to the left, and 22 percent said they were the same. This is the same response as in 1978. Washington reporters are likely to think that other Washington reporters are more liberal than they really are.

It might be possible to construct a bend-over-backwards theory about journalists' politics from the general impression that White House reporters were kinder to Republican Reagan than to Democrat Carter. My suspicion has always been that Washington journalists' likes and dislikes are based more on style than substance. For example, after a year of lunch table conversations with Senate reporters in 1984, I concluded that they liked conservative Barry Goldwater and disliked conservative Jesse Helms, liked liberal Pat Moynihan and disliked liberal Ted Kennedy.

Now, let us return to the question. Does it make any difference who covers the president? Would a different White House press corps do a better job?

As for their ability, these reporters are exceptionally experienced, averaging nineteen years in journalism, thirteen years in Washington, five years on the White House beat. They have been tested in other places. This is important for the type of daily reporting they are paid to practice. Each week they average eight stories of about 930 words each.

They have had a considerable amount of schooling for practitioners of a semiprofession that does not require advanced training for licensing or accrediting purposes, even though one could wish that their knowledge were deeper in the areas a president must be regularly involved in, such as economics. One could also wish that they were not such politicoids (a word I think I made up, meaning "resembling politicians") in that it is their habit to see every issue through a political lens. A story about competing tax proposals of president and Congress, for instance, is most likely to be shaped in terms of political winners and losers rather than in terms of what is proposed and the issues raised. The reason for this is that the reporters know more about politics than they know about tax policy. There is a political element to every presidential action, of course, but it is not the only element nor always the most important.

Unfortunately, only professional football teams can afford to have a highly trained specialist for every circumstance: a running back for first downs, a running back for third downs, and a blocking back for second and fourth. At the White House, news organizations must go with intelligent generalists.

Are they representative? When I speak of representativeness it should be obvious that I am really talking about selective representativeness. Only one in five Americans has finished four years of college, for example, but this is not a statistic people would want to see represented in those who report on the activities of the president of the United States.

Representativeness refers at root to the variables of race and sex. There are excellent reasons why a White House press corps should reflect the nation's demographics. It would say good things about the openness of the journalism business and about the position of women and minorities in our society. It would not, however, change—for better or worse—the state of reportage from the White House. Cut out the bylines on daily newspaper stories, for example, and then see if you can tell whether they were written by a man or a woman, a black or a white. I guarantee that you cannot.

This is not to say that every reporter will report every story from the same perspective. Some stories touch special sensitivities and thus demand special professional alertness. In October 1989 the Center for Media and Public Affairs published a study of abortion coverage by the *New York Times*, *Washington Post*, ABC, CBS, and NBC and found that in stories reported by men, the two sides were evenly balanced; in stories by women, prochoice outnumbered prolife views by two to one.

But reporters at the White House are given the same perspective to observe the same events. Differences among their stories largely involve writing style, and only to that degree are they "influenced by their own backgrounds" as Mark Hertsgaard contended.

If the oneness of the presidency imposes a unitary quality on its coverage, the multiplicity of characters in Congress calls for representative diversity in the Capitol Hill press corps, where reporters can and should go off in all directions. The irony of increasingly diverse congressional reporting is that it bolsters the dominance of the president in the tug-of-war between the executive and legislative branches.

To start thinking about the function performed by White House reporting, imagine the pointillist painting *A Sunday Afternoon on the Island of La Grande Jatte* by Georges Seurat. You will recall the late nineteenth-century scene: men and women strolling or sitting on the grass, flowered bonnets and parasols, top hats and walking sticks, children and dogs, even a pet monkey. And what is remarkable, of course, is that the entire scene has been constructed out of thousands of tiny dots. Now imagine that the painting is a president's term in office, *Sunday in the Park with George Bush*. Each dot represents a reporter's story. Stand close to the canvas and all you discern are dots, slightly different in shape and color; only as you move away from the canvas do the figures and the design become clear.

Does it make any difference if one reporter's dots are slightly bigger or slightly brighter than another's? The answer is no, partly because there are so many dots. But the answer also has to do with the dots.

It is June 18, 1982, a lovely late spring day in Washington, and Sam Donaldson and I are sunning ourselves outside the pressroom on the north lawn of the White House. He is describing how the three network correspondents covered Reagan's speech to the United Nations the day before. ABC and CBS had a shot of Japanese delegates examining Reagan's teleprompter. It is not important to the story, he says, but a nice touch. He notes that it was not used by NBC. CBS had the best introduction: a montage of delegates from warring countries (Israel and Lebanon, Britain and Argentina), all listening to the American president. Donaldson thinks this is classy. But the differences he outlines are like the dots that are not distinct enough to change the painting of the president. Under some circumstances, fierce competition can produce uppercut journalism; at the White House, however, competition among journalists means making sure that you never have to say you are sorry to someone back in the home office.

For Mark Hertsgaard, a radical reformer, the function of the White House press corps apparently is to expose the corruption of the presidency, as long as it is done to his specifications. For Mark Rozell, a political scientist, the function of the White House press corps seems to be to practice political science without a license, a sort of national teacher about what presidents should and should not be doing. But for mainstream media companies, who pay for reporters to be at the White House, the press corps is neither reformer nor teacher. White House reporters are there as dot makers of the presidency painting. Dot makers should not be confused with the artist. Dot makers have no scheme for the painting nor vision of how they want it to turn out in the end.

Honorable dot makers tell us what they see and hear each day and try not to tell us what they do not know. Talented dot makers tell their tales of presidents with flair, luring us into the web of their stories. Experienced dot makers keep out of traps that are set for them by the presidents' friends and enemies. They are not so remarkable that they cannot be replaced by other honorable, talented, experienced journalists. Henry Graff seems to see their role in almost mythic terms. But he is a historian and can stand back farther from the canvas. For me it is sufficient that when given their chance they do necessary and useful work.

The Golden
Triangle

I n a charming book called *An American in Washington*, published in 1961, Russell Baker wrote, "The myth that the White House is a glamorous beat impels the men who work it to behave as they conceive glamorous reporters must. . . . The State Department reporter quickly learns to talk like a fuddy-duddy and to look grave, important, and inscrutable. The Pentagon man always seems to have just come off maneuvers." The point that Baker was making, of course, is that each major beat leaves an imprint on the reporter. I agree, and here I would like to reexamine some of the institutional characteristics that I observed at the White House, Pentagon, and State Department pressrooms—the golden triangle of Washington news assignments—in 1982.

Many in the press corps at the White House arrived there by covering the winning candidate in the latest presidential campaign. This experience helps them understand presidential politics but does not ensure that they will be knowledgeable in economics or other substantive areas of presidential concern. As a result of what they know and what they do not know, they tend to interpret all presidential actions through a political lens, thus creating a form of distortion that appears to be a sharp image of reality.

From a paper delivered at a conference, "War, Peace, and the News Media," New York University, March 19, 1983; also the *Brookings Review* (Summer 1983).

At State, where tenure for reporters is longer, a different problem can occlude the perceptions of events. The lens through which these reporters refract reality is called *nuance journalism*. They portray an elaborate tango in which sources and reporters communicate with each other through glances and code words. It can be a beautiful dance when performed by experts. More often, however, there is a clumsy partner. This was particularly the way it appeared to me during the tenancy of Alexander Haig. But as more and more marginal reporters crowd the dance floor, the routine must become increasingly grotesque.

The Pentagon is the most healthy of the three beats in the golden triangle, with the most information available and the least refraction in reporters' translations. Despite recurring uproars over leaks, reporters and sources come closest to agreement on acceptable standards for what should and should not be printed or broadcast. In part this near-amity results because the regular reporters are asking the types of questions that are easy to answer, although they often appear to be more complex because they are more technical.

To put these news beats in context, it needs to be noted that only a handful of government agencies have newsrooms and a corps of regular reporters who spend part or most of each day inside specific buildings. The vast majority of agencies get only modest attention from the news media, and most government workers (including many of substantial responsibility) have merely to avoid scandal to stay out of the nonspecialized press.

Most Washington reporters work for trade publications, or cover Congress and regional news, or are on general assignment. Almost by definition the reporters permanently assigned to the White House, Pentagon, and State Department are an elite, either from the inner ring of Washington journalism (TV networks, weekly newsmagazines, wire services, and the newspapers read by so-called opinion leaders) or the top people of the middle ring (organizations willing to commit at least six reporters to covering national news from Washington).

The press corps at the White House, State, and Pentagon, mirroring the news values of the mass media, can be thought of as a ratio of 4:3:1. The Associated Press, for example, keeps four full-time reporters at the White House, three at the State Department, and one at the Defense Department.

The very small number of serious reporters at the triangle—fewer than 150, or about 10 percent of the national press corps—are relatively interchangeable. In fact, the more senior reporters may have covered two or even all three of these beats. They are not clones, of course, but much more of the differences in news coverage can be explained in terms of what is being covered than who is doing the reporting. Despite surveys that show mainstream reporters do not agree with the policy direction of Ronald Reagan (or other conservative presidents), my year of pressroom eavesdropping (more important than any interviewing) convinced me that ideology is not an overt factor in serious reporting.

Indeed, little of what reporters say to each other, day after day, has anything to do with policy. Much of their professional conversation could be fitted in two categories: that of traveler and seer. They spend so much time trailing presidents and cabinet officials around the world that a lot of their conversation revolves around such matters as the relative virtues of the VC-137 and the KC-135 (two versions of the Boeing 707 that transport VIPs). They also like to make predictions: "The Argentines won't go to war with the Brits" or "the *Daily News* is going to fold." Beyond ideology, how they are treated—a feeiing of being personally abused by certain officials—very well may influence their copy. An administration never gets the press that it thinks it deserves; it almost always gets the press that it brings upon itself.

The White House

Those whom Theodore White once called "bloodless political scientists" want White House reporters to devote more attention to writing about policy, process, management, and even organization. Perhaps they assume that this would happen if only reporters had more access to presidential advisers and the inner workings of the building. The assumption is not correct. The White House differs from every other agency of the executive branch as a news beat in that it is dedicated to covering a person. Reporters are paid to file stories about the president, not the presidency (with the exception of a couple of magazine writers). How available and forthcoming a president and his aides choose to be with the press corps can affect the quantity and quality of the coverage, but will not change its substance.

There is an almost unending stream of events staged at the White House each day for the amusement or edification of the press. Yet unless they talk to the president, it has not been a good day. "They never have enough," said Peter Roussel, a deputy press secretary. "I asked Helen [Thomas of UPI] whether it would be enough if she saw the president eight hours a day. She said no."

Reporters are increasingly assigned to the White House because they followed the president when he was a presidential candidate. TV networks, newsmagazines, and leading newspapers seem to think that a year with the winning campaign gives a reporter special connections with presidential assistants and special insights into what may be happening behind closed doors. My hunch is that this reasoning has only a surface logic. In the campaign the staff and the press corps are consumed by politics; it is the business they are both engaged in. Their levels of knowledge are not very different, and indeed, some of the senior political reporters are more knowledge-able in the arcane conventions of running for president than are many on the candidate's staff. Once in the White House, however, the most senior staff and the reporters proceed along different tracks. Aides are forced to become deeply schooled in policy matters, while, in effect, the reporters continue to do essentially what they had been doing during the campaign.

Moreover, there is a second kind of separation taking place. In the campaign the reporters and staff were supplicants to each other. The reporters' need for a story matched the candidates' need to be written about. It was a relatively reciprocal relationship and hence fairly healthy. This relationship changes once they arrive at the White House. While more often than not in Washington a political executive is a supplicant, a competitor for finite space or time in the news media, at the White House the reporters are the supplicants: They must report on the president almost without regard for whether he is doing anything or not. So as the relationship becomes more unequal, it also becomes more unhealthy.

The practical effects of the presidential-campaign-to-White-House movement are that it ensures a press corps of high energy and limited historical memory. It further accentuates politics as the touchstone that the press will use to explain the motivation of all presidential behavior. It does not ensure that the reporters will have any substantive knowledge in the two areas that they will be most often writing about—economics and international relations—because they are the two areas that presidents must most often deal with.

When the *Washington Star* went out of business in 1981, its pressroom desk at the White House was reassigned to the newspaper reporter with the next most seniority—only four years. The short tenure of White House reporters is not unrelated to the short tenure of presidents (six between 1972 and 1993—only Ronald Reagan served two full terms). If the United States starts to have two-term presidents regularly again, it might follow that there will be a cadre of more experienced White House reporters as well.

The rapid rotation of reporters to coincide with a new presidential administration has interesting unanticipated consequences. The White House beat is a catapult for the upwardly mobile reporter, primarily because it is the least specialized of the major Washington assignments. The front row of the briefing room at the White House is reserved for reporters from Reuters, ABC, UPI, CBS, AP, and NBC. On a day in late May 1982, four of the six seats were occupied by women reporters. On the same day three of the four NBC reporters were women. The most obvious reason is that in a business with a dismal affirmative action record, the White House is the assignment that (in television, especially) gets the most notice for the least hiring—since it receives the most air time—and does not require elaborate credentializing (a few months on the campaign trail will do). As a transitory assignment, women (and blacks, to a much lesser extent) then move into the competition for the other prestige jobs.

It is hardly surprising that the news medium of choice for presidents has become television. Elected officials need to reach voters; diplomats and generals do not. There were fifteen TV cameras at a bill-signing ceremony and I counted six cameras and twenty-seven people (mostly technicians) trooping into the president's office for a routine photo opportunity. The White House is the one executive agency whose news rhythm is set by TV. Conversely, the extent to which pictures now dominate the planning and timing of events makes the beat less attractive to print journalists.

What the dominance of TV means is that the White House is good for one story a day because the networks are not going to use more than one major president story on their evening news program. Thus the struggle between the press office and the pressroom is largely over what event will rise to the top each day. There are days when neither the news media nor the president makes the decision and other days when the president and the press pick the same event. It is not a closed system: both president and White House reporters are also responding to events produced by Congress, the judiciary, the opposition party, other nations, and on occasion enterprising reporters.

A real event will always displace an ersatz event, although an ersatz event can get some coverage if the president is personally involved. Given all the attention to how presidents "use" the press, content analysis will show that manufactured stories are at the margins of the news. The White House reporters forgo a lot of good stories because of how tightly limited they are to writing for the front page or its TV equivalent, but they do not often fall for the hype and the dubious.

The State Department

Unlike reporters on the White House beat, reporters at the State Department (and the Pentagon) seem to stay and stay and stay. Given the complexity of their assignments, they contend, this is most appropriate. According to Barrie Dunsmore, ABC's diplomatic correspondent, "On many beats you grow stale and rewrite. At State you keep getting better. You grow in the job. A historical memory is very valuable."

Despite the often lengthy tenure, these reporters are rarely coopted, an unfounded worry of some who write about the government-press connection. On the contrary, they are prepared, even eager, to criticize the government if they believe criticism is justified. But long tenure on a beat often means that reporters adopt the mind-set of the agency, that they increasingly approach their material from the same vantage point as those they cover.

This does not become a more serious problem because of what reporters must do and how they are treated by sources, both of which remind them periodically of their lowly journalistic status: the more important the event, the more time reporters spend waiting; the more important the story, the less frequently their calls are returned. A story the size of the Falklands crisis was almost wall-to-wall waiting. Few people had any information and fewer still would share it with the press. After six hours of phoning, NBC correspondent Marvin Kalb reached a source who said he would take one question. "How much time," Kalb asked, "until the United States expects the British to invade?" "Seven days," the source replied. The reporter thus earned ninety seconds on the evening news; in the next booth, his CBS competitor also phoned and waited, but he was not as fortunate.

The State Department and the peacetime Pentagon are essentially print beats. The Iranian hostage crisis, a TV story, was an aberration. The noon briefings at the State Department are televised, and those at the White House are not, but this does not change the basic equation; it merely gives the State Department, a talking-heads beat, an extra visual angle that may help sell a story to the producers of the evening news.

As with George Orwell's animals, reporters from the different print outlets are equal except that some are more equal than others. The State Department's paper of record is the *New York Times*: this means that foreign service officers read the *Times* first, clip the *Times*, and circulate the clips, as do the department's clients, that is, the embassies and foreign ministries. I sometimes had more than a feeling as I followed events from the government and press sides that State Department officials were negotiating with the *Times* reporters in much the same manner as they would with the diplomats of a sovereign nation. According to Joseph Kraft, for example, an important message from the 1954 Geneva conference on Indochina was leaked to the *Times* before it reached President Eisenhower's desk.

An agency's press office is the most obvious and routine part of its press relations. The great leaks do not come from press officers, and the great reporters have the least need of press officers. Yet if the press office is functioning properly, it performs a necessary service as a sort of insider's outsider and outsider's insider, chipping away at the permanent government's built-in inertia and suspicions toward the press. It also has a special importance to those reporters for whom doors are less likely to open.

The State Department had forty-two full-time press officers in Washington as of March 30, 1982. Pressroom facilities had twenty-nine partitioned working spaces, spacious offices for the AP and UPI, and six radio-TV booths. A wire service room allowed reporters access to the flowing tickers of AP, UPI, Reuters, and the CIA's Foreign Broadcast Information Service, as well as the use of a photostat machine (often out of order).

Foreign correspondents have the daily briefings piped into a comfortable lounge that the United States Information Agency maintains for them at the National Press Building, where many have their offices. Senior officials held fifty-five backgrounders in 1981, and sixteen in the first four months of 1982, open to all reporters. The State Department issued 441 press releases in 1981.

Nevertheless, of all the major government agencies in Washington, the State Department interprets its responsibility to the press most narrowly. Unlike the Pentagon, for instance, it clearly does not see its press operation as an information service. "I resent reporters asking me questions that my son could look up in the encyclopedia," said one press officer. "If a reporter wants to know how many children Sadat had, let him call the Egyptian embassy—it's not my job to tell him," said another.

The State Department is also a building full of officials with what Hodding Carter calls "old habits" in dealing or not dealing with the press. He means, as another press officer puts it, "the traditional, nineteenth century diplomatist's view is that ideally there should be no news at all." News-gathering problems are compounded, according to one person who served in the State Department during the Carter administration, because foreign service officers "see themselves as an elite and the reporters as of a lower social order. They think that foreign policy is so complicated that it can only be understood if you've passed the foreign service exam. Reporters' minds are not subtle enough. They can only botch things up and make life more difficult."

While this may be a caricature, the State Department was the only place where I found some government workers who came close to challenging the legitimacy of the press—as distinct from the usual bureaucratic tendency, which is to try to ignore the press because it is a nuisance. (The White House is different: presidential assistants are not against the press; they are only against getting a bad press.) Still, I suspect that the foreign service officers' attitude toward the press is only slightly tinged by class or caste distinctions: American reporters and diplomats get along very well when they are overseas, for instance, especially when stationed in countries that are hostile to the United States.

Rather, I think, hostility to the press partly results from this paradox: the State Department has created an elaborate news-generating system, revolving around the daily noon briefings, with great hunks of time spent each morning on the preparation of "guidances" for the spokesman, and no one knows how to turn it off, even as the foreign service officers watch themselves be swept away from the type of private diplomacy that they think is most respectable and effective.

The effort by State to keep control of diplomacy often forces reporters to search for the unverifiable. As Bernard Kalb of NBC told newcomers, "Watch out that you don't bump into a nuance." How do you spot a nuance? Reporters and officials reply that it can be identified through code words, cues, and even body language. A former State Department briefer explained, "You might say the discussions were fruitful. Or you might say that the discussions were frank. 'Frank' means that the discussions got nowhere or were hostile." Another former briefer commented, " 'No comment' means 'yes,' while 'can't confirm or deny' doesn't necessarily mean yes."

As I moved back and forth between reporters and officials, I became uneasy. Here was a "communication system" with too much room for misunderstanding, which relied too heavily on the artistic skill of those delivering and receiving messages. I was seeing too many examples of cues that were wrongly perceived. Either there were some not very good cue givers or some not very good cue takers. Or both. Even when the minutes of Secretary Haig's senior staff meetings were leaked to the *Washington Post*—they called

British Foreign Secretary Lord Carrington a "duplicitous bastard"—the reporters who covered the State Department (without claiming to know the identity of the leaker) could not agree on whether it was meant to be a friendly or unfriendly leak. Although the story was a nightmare within the bureaucracy, reporters could argue that because the minutes contained no nasty comments about the president, the leak may have been meant to strengthen Haig's hand at the White House. And as for the "duplicitous bastard" quotation, one reporter said, "Carrington can dine off that for a month!"

I asked Alan Romberg, the deputy spokesperson, to estimate the number of truly serious reporters in the diplomatic press corps. Fifteen, he said. But there were usually seventy at a noon briefing. The briefings had lured more and more of the marginal Washington reporters, many of them too inexperienced or unsophisticated for this sort of semaphore. Thus the daily sessions have become necessary if only to correct the previous day's misunderstandings.

The Pentagon

"A building breathes," said Roberto Garcia, a Brazilian journalist. "Sometimes there's more air, sometimes less." Viewed from outside, the Pentagon of early 1982 seemed to be gasping for breath. Deputy Secretary Frank Carlucci was busy administering lie detector tests to suspected leakers. Yet inside the newsroom, Pentagon reporters shrugged and mumbled something that sounded like déja vu. The press officers were more offended by Carlucci's action than were the journalists. "This is the most open place in Washington," a respected newspaper reporter told me.

"Would anyone believe you if you wrote that?"

"Reporters know it." Reporters on the beat may know it, but I found that others who drop in are always surprised.

In November 1981, Fred Hoffman of the Associated Press learned that Oman did not want a sizable landing in its territory by the U.S. Marines during a military exercise called Bright Star. His revelation infuriated the Marine Corps high command. Hoffman, who had covered the Pentagon for more than twenty years, replied, "I've never used anything that I think might endanger our security.

Obviously the Marine commandant disagrees. But we're not at war with the Omanis."

Likewise, George C. Wilson's 1982 articles that so upset Caspar Weinberger and Carlucci when they read them in the *Washington Post*—a high budget estimate, a strategy for prosecuting draft resisters—were merely embarrassments, not threats to the national security. Defense "secrets" may be harder to define than to recognize. If given a list of candidates for such categorization, my hunch is that Pentagon reporters and Pentagon officials would agree 90 percent of the time: presence or absence of nuclear weapons locations; operational deployments of ships, troops, and aircraft (except during exercises); contingency operations plans, and so forth. In this respect the Pentagon reporter is less taxed than the reporter at State, where there would be little agreement over whether that Department's stock-in-trade, diplomatic bargaining chips, are national security secrets. It is ambiguity, not patriotism, that separates reportage on these beats.

For reporters who learn to navigate the Pentagon's corridors, the very vastness of the place works to their advantage. "If someone is promoting the M-1 tank, there are plenty of people around who will tell you what's wrong with the M-1. No trouble finding them," said Richard Halloran of the *New York Times*. In most cases what you seek is there, your job is only to find it.

Some thirty-four reporters regularly move through the Pentagon corridors. They are the most specialized press corps in the golden triangle, representing such publications as *Armed Forces Journal, Aerospace Daily*, and *Air Force Magazine*. The office of the news division at the Pentagon is a large space without partitions. Reporters stand around the press officers' desks. Press officers wander in and out of the newsroom, which is across the corridor. The press office has a bank of TV sets tuned in to each network (with the sound off) and a board that lists deadlines: COB (close of business) Thursdays for *Aviation Week*; 1 p.m., *Christian Science Monitor*; 6 p.m., *Los Angeles Times*. (At the State Department the press officers and the reporters are also on the same floor, but on different corridors. Only three times in three months did I see a press officer in the newsroom. There are no TV sets or notices of deadlines in the press office. The State Department press officers' offices have doors.)

Reporters at the Pentagon are more likely to be ranked in a hierarchy based on their competency than on the medium for which they work. The reason this is possible is a remarkable daily document called *Current News*. It is nothing more than a clip sheet—most government agencies have them—but this one is so complete (45 newspapers, TV transcripts, and more than 120 magazines) and so widely circulated (7,000 copies) that it acts as an equalizer, ensuring that the reporters, regardless of whom they write for, will be read by their sources. (At State, each unit clips for its own purposes and rarely reaches beyond a handful of papers, thus furthering the inequality among news outlets. At the White House, a substantial amount of news is summarized rather than clipped, which means that its usefulness is as a quantitative assessment of what the press is covering; it is irrelevant in terms of the relationships between reporters and sources.)

Pentagon reporters in 1981–82 turned out to be the least complaining of all, and those who did complain were usually newcomers or people working for fringe operations, or both. How to explain the change from the anger and distrust of the Vietnam War years?

One theory is that things really have changed. From a military press officer: "There was so much bad blood—on both sides. We briefed every day and it was hot. *It was hot.* They didn't believe anything we said. Actually, this was good in the long run." From an experienced reporter, but not someone who had been at the Pentagon during the war: "Vietnam taught them that they can't have second-rate people in [public affairs]. These are [now] all people who could do well in other places, they're not rejects." There also have been reorganizations. Yet I doubt that changes in personnel and an improved configuration of boxes on a chart explain much.

A distinguished general, now retired, had a simpler explanation: "War is our action time." In wartime the military services close ranks, secrets become synonymous with national security, and there is less tolerance for the role of the press as critic. And, of course, unpopular wars can make the Defense Department very defensive.

Although there are times when government is less truthful, when reporters are less professional, when relations are briefly sulfuric, the typical tone of life within the press rooms of the golden triangle is more nearly sportive, of players who know the rules and are good at their positions. Most sources do not lie to reporters, but they do not tell reporters the whole truth either. The officials who usually claim to be dedicated enthusiasts of a free press really mean that they approve of a favorable press. Reporters understand this and enjoy the game.

Senators
Making News

Media coverage of senators is determined by their place in the hierarchy of the Senate, their committee membership, and their association with particular issues. And yet. . . .

Each time a newspaper story described a senator during 1984 ("Russell B. Long, a powerful, colorful and wily lawmaker. . ."), I put the clipping in a three-ring binder. Reporters often give us clues as to why they pay attention to certain senators by the words they put before or after the legislator's name. My collection of descriptive words may not explain how much news senators make, but it does suggest the characteristics that reporters find notable.

The distribution of Senate personality types—at least as depicted by the media's adjectives—resembles a bell-shaped curve. At one end of the curve is a small group of senators who might be thought of as the *originals*. From the reporters' perspective, they are the most fun to write about. Senator Daniel Patrick Moynihan of New York is described as "no stranger to melodrama," "often has displayed a flair for drama in public life," "the thinking man's hawk," "a politician known for his love of abstractions and theories." Senator Barry Goldwater of Arizona, according to press reports, has an

From *The Ultimate Insiders* (Brookings, 1986); also *Society* (January–February 1987).

"inimitable, unvarnished style" and "seems to take a perverse delight in being provocative and unpredictable, usually in pungent language."

The category of originals also included Robert Dole, Jesse Helms, Ernest Hollings, Edward Kennedy, Russell Long, William Proxmire, and Alan Simpson. (Having a stormy personal life is not what put a Kennedy or a Long in this group. John Warner and Donald Riegle, who also had unusual marital relations, did not qualify as originals.)

Originals can get as much press coverage as they want on subjects of general interest. A former Reuters editor said she sprinkled quotations from Ted Kennedy in stories because he was the one senator she could be sure that her overseas readers would recognize. Lance Morgan, Senator Moynihan's press secretary, noted that part of his job was declining requests for his boss to appear on television programs, requests that other senators covet.

Courting the press is not a factor in becoming an original. Helms did not hide his feelings about the news media or their representatives. As he told a reporter for the *Raleigh News & Observer*, "Your newspaper is a suck-egg mule." Michael Cozza, a Washington reporter for a Charlotte, North Carolina, television station, wondered whether we were on or off the record, then said, "on the record, Helms is probably the most difficult person in the Senate, other reporters will agree." The *Washington Post*'s Helen Dewar agreed. "Yet the irony is Helms is also one of the most accessible senators. It's not difficult to get him to come off the [Senate] floor to talk with you even if he won't say much." But nothing seemed to give Alan Simpson as much pleasure as arguing with a reporter who disagreed with him. I asked, "Do you need them?" He replied, "I couldn't get an immigration bill through without. . . ." (and then named four prominent journalists). Martin Tolchin told of going to Wyoming to do a story on a Simpson campaign: "In Casper, Simpson said, 'there's one editor who really hates what I stand for, always attacks me. I want you to meet him.' He then took me and the editor to dinner." Tolchin added, "Simpson is the only person in the Senate with the ego strength to take me to dinner to meet his worst critic." The Wyoming senator also developed an interesting technique for staying out of newspapers and off television when he

wanted to: he simply expressed an opinion in such barnyard language as to ensure that no reporter would quote him. ("I think the
Senate is beginning to look like a bunch of jackasses"—a comment
by Barry Goldwater—is about as gamy as an editor will permit in a
"family" news outlet.)

A sure sign that a senator is considered an original by the press is
the variety of topics on which he or she is asked to comment. (The
exception was Proxmire, whose single theme was the Golden Fleece
award for government waste.) The usual pattern is for reporters to
seek out senators because of their expertise: of the nineteen times
that Christopher Dodd was seen on the networks' evening news
programs in 1983, sixteen appearances related to U.S. policy in
Central America; of Sam Nunn's nine appearances, eight were about
U.S. military posture. But an original such as Moynihan could be
seen commenting on eleven different topics, including social security, the proposal to make Martin Luther King's birthday a national
holiday, the invasion of Grenada, a boycott of the St. Patrick's Day
parade, unemployment, U.S.-Soviet relations, the death of Senator
Henry Jackson, and various aspects of the race for the Democratic
presidential nomination. The implication was that a comment by
Moynihan, regardless of the subject, would help the story.

Few originals seem to be left in the Senate, however. Walter
Mears, a former chief Senate correspondent for the Associated Press,
remembered how in the 1960s "a quote from Dirksen or Humphrey
could carry a story." When Everett McKinley Dirksen addressed the
Senate on January 11, 1960, for example, it was to introduce
legislation to make the marigold the "national floral emblem" of the
United States. "So hardy, so lovely, so easy to grow, so diffused, so
long-blooming," declared the Senator from Illinois, "I have taken
real delight in producing a few prize marigolds." This sort of orating
is not heard anymore, according to Dennis Beal, a long-tenured
Senate press secretary. Writing in 1963, Allen Drury of *Advise and
Consent* fame recalled the "delightful characters" of the 1943 Senate,
when he was a reporter for United Press, and bemoaned the present
lot: "the suits are Brooks Brothers, the air is junior-executive." It
was a complaint heard from another generation of oldtimers in 1983,
recalling the delightful characters of 1963. It may be, of course, that
there never were many originals, just memories playing tricks.

(Congressional correspondents also seem less colorful characters than they used to be, said veterans of the Washington press corps such as Don Shannon of the *Los Angeles Times*. He recalled a reporter named Blair Moody who in 1951 went from the *Detroit News* to an appointment as a U.S. senator and on whom the reporters dropped spitballs whenever he sat in the presiding officer's chair directly below the press gallery).

Although political scientists and others claim that television has produced a new style of senator—the individualistic attention-grabber—my collection of press descriptions suggests that this view needs to be modified. Indeed, whether the suit is Brooks Brothers or not, the largest group of senators could be the *low-keys*.

> Senator Richard G. Lugar is known as a low-key, diligent, intelligent man . . . a calm and steady politician who does not indulge in temper tantrums or sarcasm . . . smart and hard-working, but he is anything but flashy.

> Senator Nancy Landon Kassebaum is a low-key, mild-mannered politician . . . more prone to study and work behind the scenes for compromise than grab headlines . . . no publicity hound.

> Senator Bill Bradley, whom friends describe as quiet and private by nature. . . . Often he speaks in a quiet monotone.

> Senator Lawton Chiles, an unpretentious lawmaker . . . a plain-spoken person who doesn't often grab headlines . . . a low-keyed Southerner.

> Senator Howard Baker . . . easygoing, conciliatory personality . . . low-key approach. . . . Those of us who have watched Howard Baker from the press gallery for the past four years might credit his remarkable success to a single quality: patience.

According to other press accounts, William Cohen, Charles Grassley, and Walter Huddleston were "easygoing"; William Armstrong, George Mitchell, and Thad Cochran were "soft-spoken"; Quentin Burdick and Carl Levin were "self-effacing"; Charles

Mathias and Paul Laxalt had "quiet charm." Others were "mild-mannered" and "even-tempered." In all, I counted thirty-four senators in this category.

Even some senators who could not be classified as low-key were said by the press to have "mellowed," notably Strom Thurmond and Bob Dole, as in the *Washington Post*: "Today the hatchet man image has faded. According to friends, Dole mellowed after marrying Elizabeth Hanford."

The group at the other end of the curve, the *volatiles*, included Alfonse D'Amato ("quick temper . . . temperamental"), Jeremiah Denton ("a sailor's tongue"), Paula Hawkins ("feisty . . . flamboyant, flip style . . . a scrappy, catch-as-catch-can sort of woman"), John Heinz ("a stubborn man with a tendency to become quarrelsome"), Roger Jepsen ("brusque"), Howard Metzenbaum ("a natural irritant"), Ted Stevens ("quick temper and stubborn nature"), Steve Symms ("eccentric"), Lowell Weicker ("volatile and voluble"), and Edward Zorinsky ("cranky").

The originals and the volatiles have certain similarities. They seem colorful compared with their colleagues in the middle, tending to be volubly opinionated and often quick to call attention to themselves. What, then, distinguishes them from each other? Not ideology or party. There are liberals and conservatives, Republicans and Democrats, in both categories. The originals, however, are more likely to have a sense of humor. When Senators Dole and Simpson were elected majority leader and whip, respectively, in late November 1984, the *Washington Post* editorialized, "they are, if not Capitol Hill's two funniest men, at least among the top five. (We mean intentionally funny, as distinct from the other kind, which abounds up there.)" The originals were also the more interesting public speakers. Reporters earn their livelihood with words, and they have a fondness for those who use language in unusual ways. Most important, the originals tend to be powerful and the volatiles tend not to be, suggesting that the distinctions reporters make among senators are largely in the eyes of the beholders, and, although they may affect the quality of a legislator's coverage, the quantity is overwhelmingly a product of position. Had Ted Stevens been elected majority leader instead of Bob Dole—he lost on a 28–25 vote—the irascible Alaska senator instantly would have been transformed from a volatile to an original, just as after Richard Lugar became chairman of the Foreign Relations Committee in 1985 a reporter discovered an occasional "glimmer of humor" that apparently he had not noticed before.

Reporters also like their senators to be a little unpredictable (it is more interesting) but not too much (it is flaky). A case in point was Charles Grassley, an Iowa Republican, whose attractiveness to the press was that he had not acted as expected. His advance billing was as a lock-step member of the New Right, so when he started to call attention to waste in the military and even proposed a freeze on military spending, he was sufficiently out of character to be newsworthy. The *Des Moines Register's* headline on a flattering profile of Grassley's first three years in office was "He'd Rather Be Right than 'Right.' "

Personality is a modest determinant of what news comes from the Senate. When I quantified the adjectives used in the *Los Angeles Times* and *USA Today* for a six-month period, personal characteristics ranked third (17 percent), behind expertise on issues (19 percent) and senators' leadership and committee positions (38 percent). But when I asked all the television network correspondents in the Senate to tell me which senators they most liked to interview, many of the names mentioned were originals, some were low-keys, and the fewest were volatiles, even though several in the latter category made a good deal of news.

Take Nancy Kassebaum and Paula Hawkins as examples. Scarcity being a factor in newsworthiness, one might think that the only two women senators would have received a lot of media attention. They did not. But Kassebaum got more than Hawkins, two-and-a-half times as much in the national media. Part of the disparity had to do with the subjects on which the senators chose to concentrate: Kassebaum (foreign policy and the budget); Hawkins (drug use and child abuse). But the greater attention paid Kassebaum probably represented a trend in national news coverage: the reaction to hype on the part of reporters was such that, all other factors being held constant, the individualistic, attention-grabbing senator (Hawkins) was at a disadvantage in appearing on network evening news and the Sunday interview programs or being mentioned in the newsmagazines and serious newspapers. When talking about Kassebaum, the

Washington Post's Dewar approvingly noted that the senator "readily admits she's not much of a [public] speaker." Journalists increasingly did not want to think that they were being sold a story, especially on Capitol Hill, which, in the words of the *Wall Street Journal*'s David Rogers, is "a big rock candy mountain for reporters."

Choosing to quote one senator rather than another also partly reflects the personal preferences of reporters. Julia Malone explained that when writing a reaction story—"What is your reaction to the bombing of the Marine barracks in Lebanon?"—after seeking out the leaders and the experts ("the mandatory types"), she based her quotations on whom she could reach, whom she had established relations with (meaning who, based on past experience, would promptly return calls), who put out statements, and who was known to have interesting (often meaning unpredictable) things to say.

Just as reporters seem to be attracted almost magnetically to certain types, other types can be counted on to repel them. Based on my press gallery conversations, I found that the repellent legislators fell into two unequal categories. Those in the smaller group were usually described as boy scouts; reporters saw a cookie-cutter sameness to their values and sometimes even to their appearance. The major criticism, however, was reserved for senators who were considered pompous, journalism's deadliest sin. Russ Ward of NBC radio mentioned two young senators who, he said, were honest, intelligent, and hardworking, but pompous. Because they were not powerful (and therefore not necessary to him), he chose other senators when he needed a quotation for filler. Dorothy Collin of the *Chicago Tribune* even had a theory about pomposity in the Senate. She thought that young senators started off pompous, mellowed in their middle years, and then returned to a pompous old age.

Senate reporters make the same choices in picking which characteristics to write about as do reporters who cover people in other lines of work. Height got mentioned if the subject was tall or short (Simpson or Baker), weight if lean or pudgy (Alan Cranston or David Boren). An unusual previous occupation (astronaut or professional basketball player) might also be noted. Deviations from the norm were what attracted attention.

Two characteristics are handled differently, however. The Senate is composed of people who are mostly handsome. One young senator bore a resemblance to Robert Redford. Looking down on roll calls from the press gallery, I counted at least twenty senators who could have posed for Arrow shirt ads. Yet in my year of underlining adjectives, I found only two senators, Roger Jepson and Barry Goldwater, described by reporters as "handsome." A senator apparently could not be declared handsome until his hair was gray, although he was more often called "silver-haired" (Frank Lautenberg, Hollings) or "white-haired." Only then did a senator look senatorial. "Although few lawmakers look more senatorial than Jepsen, the 'quality' of the handsome, white-haired senator is generally seen as his most vulnerable point," wrote a *Christian Science Monitor* reporter in January 1984. This was not a new phenomenon. Allen Drury wrote in his diary in December 1943, "Guy Gillette of Iowa and Hugh Butler of Nebraska vie for the title of Most Senatorial. Both are model solons, white-haired, dignified."

Money is the other characteristic treated in a special way. The Senate included thirty millionaires in 1984, according to one report, but only a few were regularly identified as wealthy. Those whose riches were mentioned were either associated with a brand name— "heir to the Ralston-Purina fortune"—or were "self-made millionaires." The ideologies of the Senate's millionaires also interested reporters. When I asked Howard Metzenbaum's press secretary, Roy Meyers, what adjective the senator liked to see before his name, Meyers replied, "I can tell you what he hates: 'liberal millionaire.'" ("We love oxymorons," replied a reporter.) Only once in my clippings was a senator (John Warner) described as a "conservative millionaire."

The personal characteristics that senators bring to Washington, then, do have some effect on the way they are received by the congressional press corps. But what can be said of the senators' political characteristics—where they fit along the ideological spectrum—and whether these too affect coverage?

A senator's ideology accounted for 9 percent of the adjectives used in two major newspapers in 1984. It was not Jesse Helms's personality that intrigued reporters, who were constantly searching for new terms to describe his conservatism ("fiery," "unflagging," as well as the more traditional "ultra-" and "arch-"). But would a senator be more noticed as a liberal or a conservative, Republican or Democrat?

In an earlier study I examined how the three television networks' evening news programs and twenty-two newspapers covered Congress during seven days in April 1978. The results for the Senate were that television coverage of Republicans trailed that of Democrats by 17 percent; the overall figures showed that the Democrats received 10 percent more coverage than the Republicans. Looking at what was then a Democratic-controlled Senate, I wrote:

> Some will contend that this is evidence of a Democratic leaning in the Washington press corps. Others could argue that 10 percent represents a press bonus to the majority party. Whenever a committee chairman is quoted, for example, that person has to be a Democrat. "Reporters don't care what the Republicans say simply because they're not in control," says a young Washington reporter. With Republicans taking control in 1981, the proposition should be tested.

When Congress convened in 1981 there were forty-seven Democrats and fifty-three Republicans in the Senate. (In both 1978 and 1981 Harry F. Byrd, Jr., elected as an independent, was counted with the Democrats because he received his committee assignments through the Democratic caucus.) The majority Republicans got 57 percent of the mentions on the network evening news programs during 1981–82, a 4 percent bonus. In computing the figures for 1983, I excluded all items that were about senators solely because they were considered potential presidential candidates, not a factor that would have inflated the 1978 data. There was a majority bonus, but it was not as great for Republicans as for Democrats. For Republicans it was 5 percent in 1983; for Democrats it had been 10 percent in 1978.

Senators become news—as opposed to merely being players in the drama of the Senate—when they run for president or otherwise get themselves into trouble. There were no Senate scandals in 1983, but one in 1984 illustrates how this genre gets played out in the national press. On July 23 Jack Anderson announced in his syndicated column,

> Sen. Mark O. Hatfield, whose reelection effort this year is supported by peace and nuclear-freeze groups, has used his

considerable influence to promote an oil pipeline project hatched by an international arms merchant. Hatfield, chairman of the Appropriations Committee, has continued his helpful efforts even after being warned that the Greek munitions dealer, Basil Tsakos, had a criminal record. . . .

Another July 23 article in the *Washington Post*, by investigative reporter Howard Kurtz, confirmed that Hatfield had arranged meetings for Tsakos with the secretary of energy and the president of Exxon and had endorsed the proposal to build a trans-Africa oil pipeline in conversations with the secretary of defense and the president of Sudan. The article also disclosed that Tsakos had paid Hatfield's wife, Antoinette, $40,000 in real estate fees. Hatfield said that there was no connection between his wife's real estate work for Tsakos and his support of the pipeline:

> "We have maintained very separate and distinct professional careers," Hatfield said. "She has not been involved in my political matters, and I really haven't been involved in her business."
> Hatfield said he has long been concerned that the United States is "very vulnerable to supply cutoffs in the Middle East" and faces "the great potential for a superpower confrontation" over Mideast oil. He said the pipeline could defuse the situation. . . . "That was my one and only interest in this," said Hatfield.

This was still the outline of the story when it was concluded (in the short-term perspective of the media) on August 13 at a Portland, Oregon, press conference in which Hatfield said he had been "insensitive" to the appearance of conflict of interest, and his wife said that she would donate the money she had received from Tsakos to the Shriners Hospital for Crippled Children. Between the two dates the public learned a good deal about the Hatfields' finances, Tsakos's deals, and the pipeline project, as well as the senator's thoughts on spousal rights and obligations.

A running story of this nature is usually constructed in modest increments. The actors are rarely forthcoming, and news organizations are limited in time and resources. So events uncovered become a form of a soap opera; reporters need add only one interesting new fact to what was known yesterday for there to be another episode. Thus some of the lead paragraphs:

August 8

The Senate Ethics Committee has begun taking sworn testimony in an investigation into the relationship between Sen. Mark O. Hatfield and a Greek financier who paid Hatfield's wife $40,000 for what the senator says were real estate services, according to informed sources.

August 9

Basil Tsakos, a Greek arms dealer who entangled Sen. Mark O. Hatfield and other Washington power brokers in a $15 billion trans-African oil pipeline scheme, was up to his collar in deals. For example, in February he tried to sell U.S.-made attack helicopters to the Iranian government from his Washington office in apparent violation of U.S. law, according to an intercepted cable.

August 10

When Sen. Mark O. Hatfield agreed to help Greek financier Basil A. Tsakos with plans to build a trans-African oil pipeline, he joined a long list of former government officials and corporate executives who were involved in the $12 billion project.

August 11

During a period when his wife, Antoinette Hatfield, was receiving payments from a Greek financier, Sen. Mark O. Hatfield was taking out more than a half a dozen large personal loans and selling real estate, antiques, a coin collection and other personal property.

August 13

Two former employees of Greek financier Basil A. Tsakos have charged in sworn congressional testimony that Antoinette Hatfield, wife of Sen. Mark O. Hatfield . . . performed no services for the $40,000 she was paid by Tsakos and that the senator's account of her work is "a total fabrication."

Each new "fact" must be accompanied by a reiteration of what is already known. (A newspaper or news broadcast is constructed as if the reader or listener were learning about an event for the first time.) So news stories of scandal grow exponentially until a denouement is reached, then they suddenly end. Those who followed the Hatfield-Tsakos story in the *Washington Post* and *New York Times* (combined) would have been offered the following quantity of information (including headlines, photographs, and maps):

Date	Column inches	
July 23	38	(Jack Anderson breaks story)
August 8	70	
August 9	99	
August 13	131	
August 14	116	(Hatfield's press conference)
August 15	13	
Total (7/23–8/19)	728	

After Hatfield's press conference, the press concluded (correctly) that the senator's defense was sufficient to ensure his reelection. News organizations then reassigned reporters to other stories.

There were two other middling senatorial scandals in 1984. In May, Howard Metzenbaum reported receiving a $250,000 "finder's fee" for connecting the buyer and seller of the Hay-Adams Hotel across from the White House. The only illegality alleged was that the Ohio senator may have violated a District of Columbia real estate regulation, but the District government eventually decided that he "did not act as a real estate broker or salesperson in the sale . . . [and] this matter merits no further action." In June, Roger Jepsen confirmed a story that had been reported by a Dubuque radio station, saying, according to the Associated Press, "he had visited a sex club the year before his election because he mistakenly believed it was a health spa, despite a notice on a membership application that nude encounters were offered to members."

The Iowa senator was decisively defeated in November, but neither his revelation nor Metzenbaum's were sustained national stories. The Washington press corps had never taken Jepsen seriously—"a man whose Senate term has been dogged by embarrassing incidents and maladroit statements," according to the *Wall Street Journal 's* Dennis Farney. Metzenbaum, who was taken seriously, cut his political losses by almost instantly (unlike the Hatfields) returning the money and stating, "This was a legitimate business transaction and was openly reported on my financial disclosure. It was legal. It was ethical. However, I have been in public life long enough to know that reality and perception can be easily confused."

When the Hastings Center, a think tank that examines ethical problems, was asked by the Senate Select Committee on Ethics to study possible revisions of the Senate code of official conduct, the center's scholars found that legislators bring "a measure of paranoia" to their perceptions of how the press covers questions of legislative ethics. However, they also concluded that the paranoia is not without cause, citing a CBS evening news broadcast on June 30, 1982, during which two teenage pages in the House of Representatives charged congressmen with involving them in homosexual affairs. The boys eventually recanted their stories, and FBI investigations proved that the charges were unfounded.

If 1983 was a null year for congressional scandals, and 1984's scandals were small potatoes, the Capitol Hill scandals of 1980 were extraordinary by any standards. It was a year in which eleven sitting or former members of Congress faced criminal charges or went to prison. The main scandal resulted from Operation Abscam, in which FBI agents masqueraded as Arab sheiks and seven legislators (one of whom was a senator) became enmeshed in a web of bribes. In the House of Representatives there were also two homosexual scandals, one congressman censured for financial misconduct involving campaign funds, another resigning after he pleaded guilty to defrauding the government, and a committee chairman going to jail for taking payroll kickbacks. There were several lesser scandals as well. According to a study by Timothy Cook, 1980 was the year in which the "ethical accusations" variable was the biggest single determinant of which House member was mentioned on the evening network news programs and in the *New York Times*.

Congressional scandals may happen less often than we imagine, perhaps because we tend to savor them much longer than the more mundane news from Washington, but their potential effects on politicians (including the innocent ones) add a sense of danger to the relationship between the press and Congress. They are the un-planned and unexpected in the news-producing equation. They happen because there are law enforcement agencies, political oppo-nents, and investigative reporters. They are the most unpleasant way for a legislator to make news.

The best way for a senator to be noticed by the national media is to run for president, or, if it is credible, to hint broadly of his or her availability for the job. Nearly one of every four points in my 1983 national media rating system was attributed to senators' being men-tioned as presidential contenders. If John Glenn had not sought the Democratic presidential nomination, his ranking would have dropped from first to thirteenth. Alan Cranston would have gone from second to seventeenth, Gary Hart from fifth to eighteenth, and Ernest Hollings from sixth to a forty-third-place tie with Delaware's William Roth. These four men accounted for 27 percent of all national coverage of senators in 1983, and 81 percent of their newsworthiness related to the race for the presidency. The impact of running for president had greater weight in national newspapers than on the television networks. The candidacies of Glenn, Cranston, Hart, and Hollings accounted for 12 percent of the Senate coverage on television evening news and 10 percent on the Sunday interview programs but 28 percent of the coverage by the five newspapers used for rating.

Although no senator has been elected president since 1960, the Senate is still a major launching pad for presidential contenders. The high-water mark was probably in early 1972 when ten senators, almost one-fifth of the Democrats, were being talked about as potential nominees. Four, the number of senators who sought the presidency in 1984, was more typical. Moreover, senators who lose a presidential nomination often turn up on the ticket as the candidate for vice president.

The Great Mentioner, an illusive spirit who divines which politi-cians will be considered potential presidential nominees by the news media, is an invention of *New York Times* columnist Russell Baker. "Just why The Great Mentioner mentions some names and not others is very puzzling," noted the *Washington Post*'s David S. Broder. Still, we know that the official date to start mentioning— something like a political Groundhog Day—is exactly four years before the candidates are chosen.

Thus as Democratic convention delegates gathered in San Francisco in July 1984, reporters were busy writing stories about who might be nominated in 1988. The *Wall Street Journal* carried over the names of Edward Kennedy and Gary Hart from previous lists, added Bill Bradley and Dale Bumpers as hot prospects, and included Joseph Biden and Christopher Dodd as other possibilities. Sandy Grady of the Knight-Ridder Newspapers included Hart, Biden, Bradley, and Bumpers but discarded Kennedy as "a graying lion." *U.S. News & World Report* saw Hart threatened in 1988 by "a new crop of even younger politicians—such as Senators Bill Bradley, 40, of New Jersey and Joseph Biden, 41, of Delaware." *Time* quoted retiring Senator Paul Tsongas: "The entire stable of potential candidates for 1988 comes from the new Democratic group of politicians." The magazine then commented, "Bradley, Dodd and Joseph Biden of Delaware lead the new-generation Democrats in the Senate."

That the press should have settled on Hart, Kennedy, Dodd, Bumpers, Biden, and Bradley is instructive and illustrates how the system works. Every person who enters the Senate is placed on the political press corps' mental list of potential presidents. He or she then may be crossed off. Senators can be eliminated by being too old, too stupid, too shopworn, too provincial or state oriented, or too uninterested. Being uninterested usually means that a senator has chosen to make a career in the Senate. Jews, blacks, Hispanics, and Native Americans might be put in a separate file, but probably would not be seriously considered. State size is no longer a factor; Senator George McGovern, the Democratic nominee in 1972, came from South Dakota.

If these criteria were applied to the list of Democrats in the 1983 Senate, those who survived almost exactly corresponded to the media's "early line" for 1988. Once on the list, a senator's capacity for self-promotion increases arithmetically. Ultimately, we know, the 1988 Democratic presidential nomination went to Governor Michael Dukakis of Massachusetts. But no U.S. senator lost the nomination because of lack of media attention.

I Am on TV
Therefore
I Am

During the 1980s, for a variety of reasons, including television's need to fill airtime with relatively inexpensive programming, some reporters in Washington became household names. Although celebrity was conferred upon only a handful—the Sam Donaldsons and Ted Koppels—it added an aura of power to all those who had once been lumped together as "working press" (so as to separate them from the capitalists in the front offices). That apparent power, combined with the seeming pervasiveness of the media in American life, stimulated the activities of groups with acronyms such as FAIR and AIM who were dedicated to the proposition that the biases and inaccuracies of the media are of overriding concern to the nation and must be vigorously corrected. Such organizations surely would not devote attention to a product that is unimportant. Thus by 1988 Mark Hertsgaard could assert with confidence, "The news media has become the single most influential actor on the stage of American politics."

Yet what is the importance of the media's coverage of Congress? We know that the press is important to presidents, and hence to the presidency; the nature of White House reporting is to act as a concave reflector, narrowing and maximizing attention. But Con-

From *Live from Capitol Hill!* (Brookings, 1991).

gress is 535 individuals with a jumble of interests, and reporting from Capitol Hill has the effect of atomizing the institution, separating particles of information to fit the diverse needs of legislators and news organizations. One reporter writes of legislation to regulate commodity markets, another on funding for repaving a highway through Altoona, others on other subjects.

At least since Franklin D. Roosevelt invented the fireside chat, presidents have exploited technical advances provided by the news media. Given Daniel Patrick Moynihan's Iron Law of Emulation, Congress now demands its fair share of attention. Which helps explain why legislators have hired press secretaries, allowed television cameras into committee rooms, supported the creation of C-SPAN, and expanded House and Senate recording studios. A great deal of information gets transmitted by means of these innovations. But in the end, partly because of the principle that dissemination is also dispersion, legislators can rarely concentrate enough video time or command enough newspaper space to make a difference in promoting a policy or even getting themselves reelected.

Still, not all legislators are equal. From the vantage point of the press, the House Speaker and the Senate majority leader can be handy institutional counterweights to the president. During Ronald Reagan's first term, with the Republicans in control of the Senate, Thomas P. "Tip" O'Neill suddenly became "the most televised Speaker in history." His visibility was further enhanced by his imposing physical stature, by skillful public relations help, and by Republican attempts to turn him into a campaign issue—a confluence of circumstances not likely to occur very often. Yet he appeared on less than 7 percent of the network evening news programs, whereas a president almost always gets at least one story a day.

Nor, in terms of press coverage, are all issues equal. An investigation of a Watergate or Iran-contra scandal, a debate on a Panama Canal Treaty or a resolution to go to war in the Persian Gulf, a confirmation fight over a pivotal Supreme Court appointment—all can galvanize and focus the attentions of correspondents covering Congress, although the issue is usually framed as "Will the President Win or Lose?" There are, of course, exceptions. A modest issue such as the members of Congress voting themselves a pay raise can have talk radio resonance. And there are rare legislators, a Phil Gramm or

Newt Gingrich, without seniority or previous celebrity status or even the physical attributes that are supposed to attract television cameras, who have been able to exploit the media to advance themselves and their causes. "No camera, microphone, or notebook could be too inconveniently located for Phil Gramm," recalled National Public Radio's Cookie Roberts of the Texas senator, who was ninety-ninth in seniority when he brought into being the deficit reduction law that bears his name. And Gingrich, then a junior Republican House member in an overwhelmingly Democratic body, is supposed to have said, "We are engaged in reshaping a whole nation through the news media." By 1991 his campaign had contributed significantly to the unseating of House Speaker Jim Wright and to his own election as minority whip.

That Congress does not get all the television attention it might want partly results from the nature of legislative activity: it represents the quintessential talking-heads story. The president can take the cameras to China as he walks along the Great Wall or to the beaches of Normandy for the fortieth anniversary of D Day. Even a presidential candidate can make his point from a boat in a polluted harbor. But the best a legislator can usually offer the cameras is a finger pointed at a recalcitrant committee witness. Perhaps a deeper reason for the lack of attention, however (at least until Speaker Gingrich's one-hundred-day schedule in 1995), is that Congress moves too slowly for the dailiness of American journalism or, for that matter, for the action-now psyches of most reporters. This is the pace I recorded in my Senate diary of October 5, 1984:

> Floor debate on deficit reduction plans continues. . . . Clearly everyone has already said everything, yet it drones on. It is obvious that the reporters have become bored, and, more important, that they do not have front page stories until something passes. So the impression lingers that the Senate isn't doing much. Yet it's a question of time frame. Is several weeks really too much time for cutting the budget by $149 billion over three years?

Since the studies of Joe S. Foote early in the 1980s, it has been confirmed that most legislators are seldom seen on network news.

During 1983 one-third of the members of the Senate appeared only one time or not at all on the ABC, CBS, or NBC evening news programs. Fifty-three percent of the members of the House of Representatives were never mentioned on these programs during 1986. But at the same time, virtually every journalist's and scholar's account of Congress–media relations has asserted that the situation is otherwise on local television news, where legislators have been turned into media stars in their home towns. So I looked at who appears on local television news, a strangely ignored area of inquiry, and discovered that most members of Congress also rarely get seen on these programs. Congress remains largely a print story, and as newspapers lose out to television as the news purveyor of choice for Americans, Congress loses out too.

The conundrum, then, is why television appears to be so important to the life of Congress. As researchers are finally figuring out how to measure the place of television in the political process, television's importance for Congress is best measured by the extent to which House and Senate are not covered. But members of Congress and congressional reporters do not seem to have noticed. Quite the contrary, in fact: they tend to overestimate the extent of television coverage and its importance in the legislative and electoral processes. Partly this stems from the journalist's habit of ignoring the average, the typical, and the routine. When Hedrick Smith in *The Power Game: How Washington Works* made the case for media politics as a staple of the House of Representatives by citing the activities of Stephen Solarz, Les Aspin, Richard Gephardt, and Newt Gingrich, it was as if he had chosen Larry Bird, Patrick Ewing, Michael Jordan, and Magic Johnson as representative players in the National Basketball Association. But a more important explanation is the solipsistic view of the world that permeates Capitol Hill. Reality to reporters is what they can see, to politicians what they can touch. And Capitol Hill is always crammed with cameras, lights, sound equipment, tape recorders, news conferences, handouts, stakeouts. This is their reality. This also contributes to the myth of television's power as they react to its presence rather than to its output.

The output, as I have demonstrated elsewhere, is often small. Timothy Cook has told the affecting story of Don J. Pease, a staid and hardworking backbench congressman, who wanted to extend a program of unemployment benefits that was about to expire in 1985. His staff convinced him that a visual aid was just what he needed to get himself on television:

> When his turn came up [at a rally], Pease vigorously deplored official Washington's callousness toward unemployed workers: "If you want to know the truth, the Reagan administration acts as if you don't exist." Then raising the spatula in his right hand, he shouted, "Do you know what this is? *This* is a burger flipper. This is the Reagan administration's answer to unemployment. And *you* can flip burgers all day, and *your spouse* can flip burgers all day, and you *still* won't get above the poverty line!"

The results of this exercise, according to Cook, were that the "network, evening news programs ignored the story . . . and the next morning neither the *New York Times* nor the *Washington Post* mentioned it. The staff's one consolation was a color photograph in the *Baltimore Sun*, although the caption neglected to explain why Pease was waving the spatula." The legislation did not get out of committee.

Nevertheless, Congress and its members are spending more each year trying to influence news media coverage. But the interest is not as pervasive as I had expected after reading some accounts of Capitol Hill activities. For instance, newspaper and magazine stories focus on legislators who produce electronic news releases and ignore those who do not. Press secretaries by my calculations rank a lowly fifth in the pecking order of both House and Senate offices; in the House they also spend a fair amount of time on activities that have nothing to do with the media. And perhaps one House member in five feels virtually no need to seek publicity. Jamie Whitten, who was chairman of the House Appropriations Committee, never held a press conference: "You do your job best when you do it quietly," he summarized.

Indeed, legislators should know that sound bites on the evening news will not get them reelected. Other avenues of publicity in which they can target the audience and control the message are infinitely more effective and involve less risk of losing voters. The odds of being able to move a policy debate by using television news are very long for the average member of Congress. Why then do they devote such energy to this pursuit?

One answer could be that legislators do not know of television's limited impact because it does not appear limited from their vantage point. It is limited only if the question is framed: How many impressions of me, for how long, how positively, is a voter likely to get from my effort? Rather, staff and friends collect and comment upon their appearances, thus magnifying them. (It is similar to what I witnessed a few years ago when I watched a cabinet officer reading his daily press clippings. His senses told him that an awful lot was being written about him. It was harder for him to recall that he was the only one reading all of it). Under this closed system, even an obscure cable program at an obscene hour can produce a reenforcing feedback.

Another answer could be that legislators are cockeyed optimists. Is there not some of this quality in everyone who seeks elective office? Senator William S. Cohen believed that the politicians' common denominator is ambition. "Whether it is noble or ignoble," he wrote, "it is an all-consuming passion which refuses to acknowledge the folly of its relentless pursuit." In pursuit of the elusive sound bite, surely each member of Congress thinks he is as energetic, articulate, and intelligent as Phil Gramm and Newt Gingrich. Moreover, sound-bite journalism protects legislators from themselves. Although television and newspapers work off the same definition of news, their needs differ—TV needs nine seconds, and thus must edit out redundancy and even the awkward pauses of conversational speech. This will not necessarily make legislators look good, but it keeps them from looking bad.

Add to Senator Cohen's definition of political ambition Joseph A. Schlesinger's theory of progressive ambition: "The politician aspires to attain an office more important than the one he now seeks or is holding." More than a third of the Senate once served in the House. How many senators would rather be president? On December 30, 1971, Jim Wright wrote in his diary, "In two days, a New Year will begin. It is my 50th, will be my 18th in Congress. . . . Maybe just in the past year have I really acknowledged that I won't ever be president." For some legislators, perhaps, being on television has less to do with the next election than with some future election that may only be a dream.

So, as the members of Congress supposedly rush to recording studios to tape instant reactions to the president's State of the Union message, the political pluses outweigh the minuses. Getting on the air is an advantage, even if an exaggerated one. The costs are small, both in time and money, and the money is provided by taxpayers or campaign contributors anyway. Also, because most legislators sincerely wish to be noticed, there is no longer a stigma—the show-horse label—attached to those who are exceedingly good at getting themselves on television.

Yet there is still something else. It is August 1, 1984, and I am sitting next to Senator Alan Dixon of Illinois in a screening room in the basement of the Capitol. This is part of the Senate's television complex, a railroad flat of a place carved out of long and narrow space that had once been the path of the capitol subway. There are two television studios with a control room between them, two radio studios with a control room between them, and two TV editing rooms in addition to the room where we are now watching a tape of the town meeting that the senator has recently broadcast from a cable station in Peoria. A question put to him requires a delicate answer. Dixon listens to his response. He smiles, then issues a laugh that comes from deep inside him. "I got out of that pretty good," he says. Watching a man so thoroughly enjoy watching himself is an exquisite experience. Few senators—only Moynihan and Cohen come to mind—get the same satisfaction from the printed word.

For the legislators of Capitol Hill, television is not primarily about politics at all, I realize. Or rather, without elections to be won and legislation to be passed, there would still be the rush to television. For television is about being a celebrity. Television appearances are analogues of the decor of their offices, which are filled with cartoonists' impressions of them and photographs of them taken with famous people at important events. *"The celebrity is a person who is known for his well-knownness,"* wrote Daniel J. Boorstin. In his brilliant essay, *The Image,* he concluded, "The hero created himself; the celebrity is created by the media." I am on TV therefore I am.

Leaks and
Other
Informal
Communications

n the *New York Times* on August 8, 1983, Michael deCourcy Hinds and Warren Weaver, Jr., reported,

Langhorne A. Motley, the new Assistant Secretary of State for Inter-American Affairs, told a Congressional committee last week that departmental efforts to consult with the lawmakers on Central American policy had been disrupted by "premature unauthorized partial disclosure" of plans.

"Do you mean leaks?" one member of the panel asked.

"Yes," Mr. Motley replied.

After information comes through the formal channels—press release, speech text, public document, news conference, briefing, interview, and observation of an event—reporters gather additional information through informal means that have come to be lumped together as leaks. The leak deserves a better fate than to share a common definition with rumor, gossip, and other back-channel exchanges between sources and reporters. As defined by Motley, a leak is a "premature unauthorized partial disclosure," as distinguished from a "premature authorized

From *The Government/Press Connection* (Brookings, 1984); also *Society* (January–February 1985).

partial disclosure," which is a plant. Or, depending on one's vantage point, a plant is a beneficial leak.

The leak is rarely a tool of press offices, whose domain is the formal channels of information. Robert Pierpoint of CBS says that during the six presidencies he covered, a White House press secretary only once leaked information to him. The primary reason spokespeople try to stay out of the leaking business, according to former presidential press secretary George Reedy, is that "since manipulation of the press involves favoritism to some newsmen, it inevitably creates antagonism among others."

Nor is leaking often practiced in the lower civil service. The bureaucrats' world faces inward. They know best how to maneuver within their own agencies; journalists, except possibly for some specialized reporters, are outside their ken and represent risk beyond possible gain.

The U.S. Constitution, however, provides reporters with a legislative branch in which they can always find someone who will enjoy sharing the president's secrets with them. John Goshko, who reports from the State Department for the *Washington Post*, recalls that a good story came from a congressional staff member who was talking to a *Post* congressional reporter, Margot Hornblower, who then told Goshko. "When the congressional staffer read the story he could never have known that he was the source," says Goshko. According to a wise departmental press officer, "we just assume that anything given to the Hill will be leaked and act accordingly." It is a painful lesson for presidents to learn. President Reagan briefed his leaders in the House and Senate on what would be in his State of the Union message and the next day read David Broder's story on the front page of the *Post*: "Neither [Howard] Baker nor [Robert] Michel would elaborate on the contents, preserving the secrecy the White House hopes to maintain until Reagan gives his address to Congress and the nation next Tuesday. But sources on Capitol Hill said it would probably include. . . ."

The greatest frustration for presidents may be when they are forced to realize that most executive branch leakers are their own people—political appointees—rather than the faceless bureaucrats they campaigned against. "A government," as James Reston was first to note, "is the only known vessel that leaks from the top."

From the journalists' point of view, wrote Tom Wicker in the *New York Times*, "What Presidents are apt to consider leaks . . . are often more nearly the result of good work by reporters diligent and intelligent enough to ask the right questions of the right sources at the right time." Former Secretary of State Dean Rusk, quoted in the *Foreign Service Journal*, offered a hypothetical example of how the process can work:

> A reporter is leaving the State Department at the end of the day when he sees the Soviet ambassador's car drive up. Figuring that the ambassador has brought a message, the reporter gives the machinery a chance to work, then starts calling around. After being told he's on the wrong track at several offices, he gets to the fellow on Berlin, who has been told never to lie directly to the press. The reporter says, "John, I understand that the Soviet ambassador has just come in with a message on Berlin." So the man says, "Sorry, I can't say a thing about it. Can't help you on that." Ah! He's got it. In the absence of an absolute denial, he's on the track. He figures out what the Berlin problem looks like and then calls a friend at the Soviet embassy. "By the way," he says, "what's the attitude of the Soviet Union on this particular point on Berlin?" He listens for a few moments, then he [writes] his story [for] the next morning on the message the Soviet ambassador brought in about Berlin.
>
> The chances are that the president will call the secretary of state and ask, "Who in the hell has been leaking news over at the Department of State?"

It is a "curious delusion among upper bureaucrats and high officials," Stewart Alsop concluded in 1968, "that a reporter cannot possibly reach the same rather obvious conclusions that government officials reached unless the reporter has had illicit access to secret information."

Viewed from inside government, a typology of why leakers leak would include:

The Ego Leak: giving information primarily to satisfy a sense of self-importance; in effect, "I am important because I can give you information that is important." This type of leak is popular with staff, who have fewer outlets for ego tripping. Assistants like to tell (and embellish) tales of struggle among their superiors. I believe ego is the most frequent cause of leaking, although it may not account for the major leaks. Other Washington observers disagree. Many reporters and officials prefer to think of leaks as more manipulative and mysterious, but this also serves their egos.

The Goodwill Leak: a play for a future favor. The primary purpose is to accumulate credit with a reporter, which the leaker hopes can be spent at a later date. This type of leak is often on a subject with which the leaker has little or no personal involvement and happens because most players in governmental Washington gather a great deal of extraneous information in the course of their business and social lives.

The Policy Leak: a straightforward pitch for or against a proposal using some document or insiders' information as the lure to get more attention than might be otherwise justified. The great leaks, such as the Pentagon papers in 1971, often fit in this category.

The Animus Leak: used to settle grudges. Information is disclosed to embarrass another person.

The Trial-Balloon Leak: revealing a proposal that is under consideration in order to assess its assets and liabilities. Usually proponents have too much invested in a proposal to want to leave it to the vagaries of the press and public opinion. Most likely, those who send up a trial balloon want to see it shot down, and because it is easier to generate opposition to almost anything than it is to build support, this is the most likely effect.

The Whistle-Blower Leak: unlike the others, usually employed by career personnel. Going to the press may be the last resort of frustrated civil servants who feel they cannot correct a perceived wrong through regular government channels. Whistle blowing is not synonymous with leaking; some whistle blowers are willing to state their case in public.

Leaks can be meant to serve more than one purpose, which complicates attempts to explain the motivation behind a particular leak. An ego leak and a goodwill leak need not be mutually exclusive; a policy leak also could work as an animus leak, especially since people on each side of a grudge tend to divide along policy lines; and all leaks can have policy implications regardless of motive.

Beyond the basic leaks, experienced reporters and officials enjoy trying to identify elaborate variations, such as "the daring reverse leak, an unauthorized release of information apparently for one reason but actually accomplishing the opposite," an invention of Hugh Heclo. A candidate for this distinction was Bob Woodward's *Washington Post* story on February 19, 1982, that reported on notes taken by a participant in Alexander Haig's senior staff meetings. Among the revelations were that the U.S. secretary of state called the British foreign secretary, Lord Carrington, a "duplicitous bastard," and that in private Haig had a much grimmer assessment of U.S. prospects in the Middle East than he had in public. Most initial reaction was that the notes had come from someone who was out to get Haig. But on February 22, William Safire presented an alternative suggestion in his *New York Times* column: Woodward was investigating a disturbing question—"Was it true that Al had gone bonkers?"—and the leaker was a Haig loyalist who felt a plausible selection of notes could show that his boss was of sound mind and in command. Former State Department spokesman Robert McCloskey, who had become the *Post*'s ombudsman, wrote that the leak was "dishonorable" and that the leaker was a "villain." If Woodward knew "whether the source's motive was benign or mischievous. . . [he] had an obligation to share it with the reader." The reporters I interviewed, however, argued that the leaker's motivation need not concern them, only whether a story is true.

A year later, Safire's theory had become the conventional wisdom in Washington. Correct or not, it undoubtedly will be a permanent and cherished addition to the insiders' mythology of leaks. But few reporters, officials, or scholars ever mention "the no-purpose leak," based solely on the gregarious nature of politicians. Or as one congressional reporter put it, "on the Hill they talk because they love to talk."

The winter of Ronald Reagan's discontent with the press began in late October of his first year in office, a bit delayed in historical terms because of the March 30 assassination attempt. Understanding all the major battles that were fought through the press during the turmoil of November and December 1981 and January 1982 gives us a better sense of the uses of leaks and other informal means of communication than if special cases had been chosen. The period coincides with the fine-tuning of the president's annual budget proposals in a mid-term election year, always a busy time for intrigue. Although not typical in intensity, these months do reflect the standard array of conflicts that are reported from Washington, beginning with high-level personality clashes.

On October 27, 1981, Joseph Kraft wrote in the *Washington Post*:

> Among the rumors of change, one features a grand game of musical chairs: Meese for Defense in place of Weinberger, who then takes Haig's place at State, with Haig's deputy—William Clark, a former Reagan aide in California—moving to the White House in place of Meese and Allen.

The next day, Bob Schieffer reported on the *CBS Evening News*:

> Although White House spokesmen won't confirm it, one scenario being discussed in the back channels has top White House aide Ed Meese eventually being shifted to the Pentagon to replace Defense Secretary Weinberger, who would shift to State to replace Secretary Haig. White House National Security Adviser Allen would be assigned duty elsewhere. His post would either be reduced in rank or, perhaps, filled by a career foreign service officer, such as Philip Habib.

The president was obviously annoyed. As reporters walked with him across the White House lawn to a waiting helicopter on October 29, he said that Kraft and Schieffer were "blowing smoke [and] also doing a disservice to this country. I am very happy with the team we have . . . we're all getting along fine, and there's going to be no musical chairs being played."

Rumors of such a high order, popping up simultaneously in two major news outlets, "are almost always intended to damage the political fortunes or alter the policy views of the chosen victim," *New York Times* reporter Leslie Gelb noted several days later, "and they are almost always untrue—at least when first disseminated." The beauty of the musical-chairs rumor was that it was aimed at both the national security adviser and the secretary of state. Thus it reflected the hostility of almost everyone in Washington. Those who were against either Haig or Allen included most of the White House, State Department, Pentagon, and Congress. Yet the rumor was too grand to be anything but the talk of White House corridors. That it eventually turned out to be semi-accurate—Haig and Allen were removed from public life within a year—needed a great deal of assistance from the two men. Allen obliged his critics by having been shown to have accepted $1,000 and several watches from a Japanese magazine as a thank-you for arranging an interview with Mrs. Reagan. The revelations led to his departure from government, but that departure was not related to institutional, personality, or policy disputes with the secretary of state. Haig's problems within the administration were of a different order.

On Saturday afternoon, October 31, David Gergen at the White House obtained an advance copy of a syndicated column that was scheduled to appear on Tuesday, November 3, in which Jack Anderson put Haig's name on the top of the president's "disappointment list." According to unnamed White House sources, "the secretary of state reportedly has one foot on a banana and could skid right out of the Cabinet before summer." As the administration's director of communications, Gergen phoned Anderson to request a disclaimer in that the president had repeatedly said he retained confidence in his secretary of state. Gergen then told Haig about the impending column.

Haig called Anderson twice during the day. He was "angry and upset," said the columnist, and indicated that the attack on him "was obviously the handiwork of a top White House aide, who had been running a guerrilla campaign against him for nine months." Anderson then rewrote his column to include this new information. Anderson's wide readership and the type of exposé that he specializes in give him some influence. But unlike the chief diplomatic correspondent of the *New York Times*, secretaries of state need not notice Anderson in order to perform their stately duties nor do embassies cable the muckraker's views to their foreign ministries. However, the State Department, through its spokesman, confirmed that Haig was accurately quoted, which ensured that the Anderson column would be noticed by media powers and the foreign ministries that are important to a secretary of state.

On November 4 a front-page headline in the *New York Times* announced, "Haig Charges a Reagan Aide Is Undermining Him." Between the headline and Bernard Gwertzman's story, there was also a three-column photograph of Reagan, Haig, and Allen. The *Washington Post* had the story on page 1 for two days (Anderson's column was on page B15). The *Post* articles by Don Oberdorfer and Martin Schram rehearsed in detail the conflict between Haig and the White House staff since the president's inauguration, including, most recently, that Haig had confronted White House Chief of Staff James Baker about the Schieffer and Kraft stories. The reporters concluded, "the disputes, at times occurring publicly, seemed to be personal infighting rather than struggles over ideology."

The "Guerrilla Campaign Controversy," as it was called by the *Post*, was still on the front page when Haig became embroiled in another dispute. Testifying before the Senate Foreign Relations Committee, he said, "there are contingency plans in the NATO doctrine to fire a nuclear weapon for demonstrative purposes." The statement was an aside, meant to illustrate a point. The next day, November 5, the secretary of defense, testifying before the Senate Armed Services Committee, replied, "there is absolutely nothing in any of the plans with which I am familiar that contains anything remotely resembling this, nor should be." Responding to Senator John Warner, Republican of Virginia, Weinberger was clearly expecting the question. By late afternoon, David Gergen resolved the matter: "Both were correct fundamentally." Film clips of Haig and Weinberger, separated by a twenty-six-word bridge on the *NBC Nightly News*, created a compelling drama.

The president summoned Haig and Allen to the Oval Office on November 5, just as he would shortly have to summon David Stockman: "going to the woodshed," Stockman called the experience. In both cases Reagan emerged to blame the press. "Sometimes I wonder if there is such a thing as an unnamed source," said the president, using his more-in-sorrow voice. Columnist William Safire replied:

The truth, as any Washington reporter will attest, is that it is hard to avoid being buttonholed by high White House aides complaining about the turfbuilding Mr. Haig, or by State officials running down Richard Allen and (more gingerly) Defense Secretary Weinberger. . . . These sources are neither "sinister forces" nor "unnamed"—they may be unidentified, but they have real names—and are not figments of journalistic imaginations, as Mr. Reagan suggested.

The *Chicago Tribune*, noting that the "public whining of some of the president's top foreign policy officials is becoming a disgrace," lectured the foreign policy establishment to "stop this infantile wrangling."

Less than a week later, on November 11, new shock waves hit the administration when advance copies of the December issue of the *Atlantic* arrived in Washington. Its lead article was "The Education of David Stockman" by William Greider. Stockman, a former Republican congressman from Michigan, had been appointed to his cabinet-level job as the director of the Office of Management and Budget after pledging public fealty to supply-side economics; Greider was an assistant managing editor of the *Washington Post*. For more than eight months the conservative official and the liberal journalist had been meeting, and there were eighteen tape-recorded interviews to prove it. The length of the article, nearly 18,000 words, guaranteed that most people would learn its contents from news reports. Reporters, naturally, highlighted the most unexpected Stockman quotations. "None of us really understand what's going on with all these numbers," he said about the president's budget. Later he said that the Kemp-Roth bill, the president's tax proposal, "was always a Trojan horse to bring down the taxes that the rich must pay. . . . The rest of it is a secondary matter." On the bargaining that produced the tax legislation: "Do you realize the greed that came to the forefront? The hogs were really feeding." Could Stockman have been misquoted or sandbagged by a wily adversary? The November 12 headline in the *New York Daily News* read, "Stockman Is Mugged by Mag." No, said Stockman, Greider had not acted in bad faith. "In early September, at our last meeting," Greider later wrote, "I again reminded him that I was preparing to publish the full account of our conversation, and again he assented."

Greider said that as an editor he was getting "a valuable peephole on the inner policy debates of the new administration," but what did

Stockman expect to gain? Greider said he assumed Stockman felt he was getting "a valuable connection with an important newspaper . . . [that he could use] to prod and influence the focus of our coverage." If so, it turned out to be a bad deal for the president, who, after all, had not been a party to the bargain.

Once again the wounds of an administration were self-inflicted. Presidents have a right to try to conduct their internal business in an orderly manner and to try to time their moves to their advantage. This need not be of high concern to reporters, but the cabinet and the White House staff are a president's employees, presumably expected to be loyal and discreet. When leaving the administration in December 1981, Reagan's political adviser, Lyn Nofziger, said, "It seems to me that some people in talking to the media forget that when they are putting out information that may be hurtful to another member of the Administration, that what they are doing is hurting the President."

On December 3 James McCartney wrote in the *Philadelphia Inquirer* under the headline, "Force in Central America Opposed": "Haunted by memories of Vietnam, the Defense Department is strongly opposing White House and State Department threats to use military force to halt what the administration perceives as subversion by leftist forces in Central America." McCartney, a veteran on the national security affairs beat, was surprised that this was the lead story in the Defense Department's early bird news clips. It was not new news, he readily admitted. Leslie Gelb had a front page story in the *New York Times* a month earlier in which Haig was said to have "been pressing the Pentagon to examine a series of options for possible military action in El Salvador and against Cuba and Nicaragua," while the military was said to be opposing military action. Also on November 5, just after the president had told Haig and Allen to stop squabbling, Hedrick Smith of the *Times* had an interview with the secretary of state in which he "indirectly confirmed" Gelb's story.

Given all the talk of military options, McCartney had gone to the Pentagon to ask very specific questions about matters like "interdicting supplies." Instead he was directed to "a certain guy who volunteered to flesh out my questions into a 'broader perspective.'" McCartney later said, "He was answering questions I hadn't asked."

The Defense Department wished to advertise a policy disagreement with the State Department. This was not a personal feud. McCartney noted, "They hadn't tried to sell me a story in the first place." He walked through the door and they saw an opportunity to make a pitch for their position. His article led off the Pentagon news clips on December 3 partly because copies of the *New York Times* happened to arrive late; being in the early bird edition attracted the attention of other reporters, who told me they planned to write stories about the dispute.

Another story, "U.S. Search Is on for 5 Terrorists Reported Planning to Kill Reagan," was reported by Philip Taubman on December 4 in the *New York Times*: "The Government has received detailed reports that five terrorists trained in Libya entered the United States last weekend with plans to assassinate President Reagan or other senior Administration officials." This account, along with similar reports from ABC and *Newsweek*, began a month of charges and countercharges. The stories reminded the *New York Daily News* Washington bureau chief, Lars-Erik Nelson, of a Robert Ludlum thriller; there were even claims of two hit squads equipped with missiles that could shoot down Air Force One or destroy the president's limousine. "Live and by satellite," Libyan leader Muammar el-Qaddafi appeared on *This Week with David Brinkley* to say that the president of the United States was "a liar" and "silly." Mr. Reagan retorted, "We have the evidence and he knows it." The Senate Foreign Relations Committee was called into session to be briefed by the FBI. The Senate Intelligence Committee was briefed by the CIA. The president twice convened the National Security Council. The government asked all Americans to get out of Libya and announced a ban on travel to that country. It was never clear that hit squads had actually entered the United States, FBI director William Webster said later, but the evidence deserved to have been taken seriously at the time.

Where did the leak come from? The White House? The State Department? FBI? CIA? Secret Service? Why would each or any of these organizations have an interest in publicizing the information? These were questions that fascinated Washingtonians. On rival op-ed pages, two well-connected columnists tried to solve the riddle.

THE USES OF PUBLICITY by William Safire *New York Times* December 10, 1981	THE LIBYA WEEK by Joseph Kraft Washington Post December 10, 1981
The input from the Haig junta on the Seventh Floor of the State Department, I assume, would be to use this provocation to escalate the war of nerves with Libya. From our diplomatic point of view, publicity about the export of terrorism is desirable.	High State Department officials, when they learned of the Libyan hit squad story, were concerned that publication might upset the delicate African operation [to get Libyan troops out of Chad]. So the foreign policy logic, far from pushing for a public confrontation with Qaddafi at this time, argued that it was far better to keep mum.
Someone in intelligence must have supported that hope for secrecy, holding that publication of our knowledge of the plot would blow sources and methods.	The stories all appear to come from the intelligence–cum–law–enforcement community. . . .
Finally, the view from the White House: . . . the case for publicity rather than secrecy is overwhelming.	President Reagan was, accordingly, enraged by the leaks.

Another *Rashomon*-in-Washington effect was churned up by a story spread across the front page of the *Washington Post* on February 14, 1982: "Reagan Backs Action Plan for Central America." Reporters Don Oberdorfer and Patrick E. Tyler credited "informed sources" and "reliable sources" with revealing a long list of actions that were being discussed at the highest levels of government, including "a secret $19 million plan to build a broad political opposition to the Sandinista rule in Nicaragua, and to create 'action teams' for paramilitary, political operations and intelligence-gathering in Nicaragua and elsewhere." Three syndicated columns then produced three totally different theories to explain the who and why of the supposed leak. Flora Lewis wrote in the *New York Times* about "amateur leakers" in Washington, "people whose aim is not so much to manipulate the daily course of events as to blow the whistle on abuse, deceit, wrongheadedness that they have come to find intolerable and impossible to stop through government procedures." The *Post* story, she concluded, was "evidently leaked to blow a whistle." Rowland Evans and Robert Novak believed there was nothing amateurish about the leak. They suspected White House operatives whose rationale was that the president would "suffer politically" if the United States intervened in Central America, and therefore they wanted to set off "a public reaction" against the plan. "The White House undermined its own plan," contended the columnists. Finally, Georgie Anne Geyer suspected that the administration planted the story to use "the threat of covert warfare and activity as an overt military threat." This is why, she concluded in the *Washington Times*, "the administration's 'anger' over the supposed leaks was barely halfhearted." The three theories are logical, internally consistent, and interesting. They cannot all be correct; possibly all are wrong. Strangely, when it is not their story, reporters who have themselves worked Washington's informal channels of communication often assume that a leak has a single source or a single cause or both. That assumption is most often accurate when a specific document is leaked, but this did not appear to be the case in either the Libyan hit squad or Central American covert operations stories.

It was expected that the president would announce whether there would be a new tax proposal when he delivered his State of the Union message on January 26. Prospects that taxes might go up were suggested by Edward Cowan's story in the *New York Times* on January 7: "President Reagan's economic advisers have reached a consensus that he seek increases in 'consumption taxes,' including those on alcohol, tobacco and gasoline, as part of a strategy to shrink budget deficits in the next few years well below $100 billion." This story was particularly notable because of the president's long-held opposition to an increase. An explanation of the internal maneuvering within the administration was given in the *Times* on January 8 by White House reporter Steven R. Weisman:

> White House officials have been working hard in recent weeks to achieve unanimity among themselves on the need for at least some tax increases in 1983 and 1984. Their assumption has been that only with a unified approach could they hope to persuade a reluctant Mr. Reagan to accept tax increases to help reduce the Federal deficit.

Press Secretary Larry Speakes reminded reporters that "nobody knows [what Reagan will do] except the man in the Oval Office," and the president "doesn't look with favor on new taxes." David Gergen told reporters that the president did not want to decide in a fishbowl of public attention, and asked his aides to stop speculating about what he was going to do.

A lead story in the *Times* on January 21 announced that the "President's [pro-taxes] decision . . . came at a White House meeting with senior officials this afternoon." The next day Howell Raines wrote, "President Reagan appeared to be having second thoughts today," and that the *Times* story on the previous day had caused "speculation and suspicion in the Reagan inner circle as to who had leaked it." Another January 22 *Times* article, by Steven Weisman, claimed that "the President's jocularity about [the leaks] has given way to anger. That is apparently the tone he took today reading the latest reports of his approval of tax increases."

President Reagan did not propose a tax increase in 1982. The stories tended to be wrong in tone even though they contained strong disclaimers, that is, they stressed that the president would probably support new excise taxes but that no decision had been made and the president did not like the idea. No one denied, however, that the articles correctly reflected the views of the majority of Reagan's top advisers at the time they were written. Columnists Evans and Novak contended that the president's aides—the White House chief of staff, the director of the Office of Management and Budget, the secretary of the treasury, and the chairman of the Council of Economic Advisers—were using the news media to pressure him in a "game of decision-by-leak." If so, it was a strange strategy. The stories were not designed to rally public support. Why should Reagan have looked favorably upon more excise taxes because they had been reported in the *Times* and elsewhere? Indeed, given his irritation over leaks, the articles could have been expected to be counterproductive. They gave opponents of tax increases, such as the U.S. Chamber of Commerce, an opportunity to apply counterpressure.

Miscalculations by those who leak about what they think they are accomplishing should never be underestimated, but this flurry of leaks was more likely caused by an exceptionally large number of major figures in the executive branch and the Congress, all with staffs, interacting with a lot of reporters. An experienced *Times* reporter commented, "Most so-called leaks simply result from calling a source, and if I can keep him on the phone long enough, he'll say something, maybe just to get rid of me. It takes a certain skill [for an official] to say nothing, not to be afraid of being a bore."

The *Washington Post*'s Pentagon reporter, George C. Wilson, reported on January 8, "Pentagon executives were warned yesterday that President Reagan's plan to rearm America, as interpreted by the Joint Chiefs of Staff, could cost up to $750 billion more than the administration has earmarked over the next five years." The warning was made "in a report presented at yesterday's [Defense Resources Board] meeting by Richard D. DeLauer, head of weapons research and procurement." Wilson quoted liberally from the secret report and added, "a Pentagon executive who was at the Resources Board meeting confirmed that the whole purpose of the session was to bring about greater realism in projecting how much the Pentagon can afford to buy between now and the end of the decade."

Later, when asked to investigate the Defense Department's investigation of the leak, the General Accounting Office noted that there were twenty-four principal participants at the January 7 meeting, including the deputy secretary of defense, two under secretaries of defense, the secretaries of the army, navy, and air force, and the Joint Chiefs of Staff. There were also staff members assisting in the briefing, staff members with access to the briefing books, and other staff members who were debriefed after the meeting.

On the day Wilson's article appeared, Deputy Secretary Frank Carlucci initiated an investigation that, according to the GAO report, would "set a precedent with respect to the level and number of officials involved." The Pentagon's second-ranking official must have been particularly upset that the reporter was calling around to verify his information within two hours after the Defense Resources Board meeting adjourned. Carlucci volunteered to take a lie detector test to determine whether he had been the leaker and urged others to do likewise. One participant complained, "It is . . . like asking someone to volunteer for root canal work." By January 12 the lie detector had been used on thirteen individuals; twenty-six people were eventually polygraphed.

Because the administration was just wrapping up the 1983 fiscal year budget with a substantial increase for defense, it was more than routinely sensitive to talk of underestimated weapons costs. Secretary Weinberger promptly told CBS that he had not "the slightest intention" of approving the higher figure. Wilson had reported "simply a wish list and nothing more."

The polygraph investigation story appeared in the *Washington Post* on January 13. Asked about what had initiated resorting to lie detectors, Henry E. Catto, assistant secretary of defense for public affairs, responded at his regular briefing on January 14:

Well, I certainly wouldn't for a minute say that the particular DRB meeting dealing with budget is likely to endanger national defense. . . . It's the principle of the thing that we strenuously object to, the expression of minority opinion via leaks to the news media designed to influence the course of events. We feel that things ought to be decided in camera and then a policy supported by everyone who stays on the team.

In a later interview with Wilson, Catto added, "if you all thought that every editorial board meeting of the *Washington Post* was going to be on the front page of the *Journal* or the *Times* the next day, it would inhibit your freedom to plan and discuss what stories you're going to work on. It would be a difficult situation, and that's the situation we're in." At the same time, stories about the investigation received more attention than the story that had set off the investigation.

In April the Pentagon revealed that it had found the leaker and he would be dismissed. The accused was John C. F. Tillson, director of manpower management in the Office of the Assistant Secretary of Defense for Management. He had flunked three lie detector tests. At this point Wilson, sixteen years on the defense beat, sent a letter to the secretary of defense: "An honorable man stands falsely accused. . . . I give you my word, John was in no way connected with the story I gathered and wrote." The Pentagon then reprimanded Tillson, whose lawyer was quoted in the *Post* of May 20 as saying that this was a "complete vindication, although I would rather have seen them send him a letter of apology." The subsequent GAO report said that the Defense Department had conducted sixty-eight investigations into the leaking of classified information since January 1975, and "in no case was there any indication that an individual was removed from a position of trust because of an investigation. In most cases, the sources of the leaks could not be determined because of the wide dissemination of the classified information."

On May 27, as the result of another leak, Wilson reported that a "secret Pentagon planning document makes clear that the administration has no intention of filling what in the past it has dismissed as the military's 'wish list.' " This, too, was classified information, but Secretary Weinberger apparently did not find this leak objectionable.

The story on the decision not to sell jet fighters to Taiwan was reported by Don Oberdorfer in the *Washington Post* on January 11:

> The Reagan administration, seeking to avert a falling out with the People's Republic of China, has decided against selling new high performance jet fighters to Taiwan. . . . There is no doubt that Taiwan and its backers in the United States would be sorely disappointed by the administration's decision. Ronald Reagan long had been counted as a special friend of Taiwan based on close ties before his election to the presidency.

This story was cited at the White House on January 13 when Larry Speakes explained the administration's plan to crack down on leakers. "We do think it did not allow us to conduct foreign policy in an orderly manner," he told the noon briefing. "We were in the process of consulting with allies and we were in the process of consulting with members of the Congress, and this appeared in the press before this consultation process was completed."

Oberdorfer and other diplomatic correspondents had been expecting an announcement on the sale, but they did not know when. The *Post* reporter was to have had an appointment with John Holdridge, assistant secretary of state for East Asian and Pacific affairs, on Friday, January 8, which Holdridge's secretary canceled at the last minute. Holdridge had laryngitis, she said. Unlikely, thought the reporter. On Sunday, Oberdorfer was listening to the evening news on ABC, when Jack Smith reported the decision on the Taiwan jets. "The minute I heard it I knew it was right," Oberdorfer later told me. "I was piggybacking off ABC, but since nobody in this town watches, it never happened." The *Post* reporter then started phoning until someone reacted, "My God, the President said that this one must be held close to the chest." Oberdorfer wrote the paper's lead story at his dining room table without having had to leave home.

Jack Smith says he got the initial tip on the story from another reporter who was peeved that his editor did not think it was important. Smith worked Friday and Saturday. His operation did not think much of the story either, holding it over from Saturday night to Sunday night and even then using it in the second half of the program. Smith's report was less specific than Oberdorfer's. Still the ABC correspondent said he felt a little out on a limb and was relieved when he saw the *Post's* front page on Monday. Smith later said, "It occurred to me to ask [his key source] whether this story endangered U.S. policy or compromised it in any way. I was told that it didn't. If the answer had been otherwise, I was prepared to make a strong case to my editor not to use the story at that time."

On January 12, at a hastily called briefing in the early evening, a spokesman delivered a statement from the president:

> Unauthorized disclosure of classified information under the jurisdiction of the National Security Council and of classified intelligence reports is a problem of major proportions within the U.S. Government. The Constitution of the United States provides for the protection of individual rights and liberties, including freedom of speech and freedom of the press, but it also requires that Government functions be discharged effi-

ciently and effectively, especially where the national security is involved. As President of the United States, I am responsible for honoring both constitutional requirements, and I intend to do so in a balanced and careful manner. I do not believe, however, that the Constitution entitles Government employees, entrusted with confidential information critical to the functioning and effectiveness of the Government, to disclose such information with impunity. Yet this is precisely the situation we have. It must not be allowed to continue.

The statement went on to establish specific policies. The president directed that "all contacts" with reporters in which classified information was to be discussed would require the "advance approval of a senior official" and must be followed by a memorandum outlining "all information provided to the media representatives." Fewer officials would have access to intelligence documents. "In the event of unauthorized disclosure," officials would be investigated and the investigations would "include the use of all legal methods." Although the spokesperson, David Gergen, insisted that there had been a string of damaging national security leaks, he cited only Oberdorfer's story. However, as if to underline the administration's concern, on January 13 the *Post* ran a story headlined "Crates of Soviet Aircraft Detected Near Havana." Some officials were to contend that this caused the crates to disappear suddenly and also may have revealed the accuracy of U.S. satellite cameras.

Nevertheless, the reaction from the press to Reagan's directive was swift. The head of the State Department Correspondents Association, Barrie Dunsmore, attacked it as having a chilling impact on sources. Jack Landau, executive director of the Reporters' Committee for Freedom of the Press, said he could see "no other reason for the White House to look over the shoulder of every policy maker who talks with the press except to make sure that whatever information gets out makes the administration look good." Columnists and editorialists joined in the criticism.

Inside the government, press officers Gergen, Benjamin Welles (Defense), Alan Romberg (State), and Jeremiah O'Leary (National Security Council) argued "vehemently" with National Security Adviser William Clark against the proposed directive, O'Leary wrote after he returned to journalism. On February 2 Clark issued new procedures that White House officials said were meant to supersede the January 12 presidential order. The revision omitted any reference to the control on interviews. It left out the threat to use "all legal methods" to pinpoint the sources of leaks. Instead it focused on that part of the original directive meant to limit the number of people with access to classified data. White House officials admitted that the new policy was now pretty much a reiteration of the old policy.

At a news conference on January 19, 1982, President Reagan declared that leaks had "reached a new high." Although the *Sporting News* does not keep administration-by-administration statistics, his claim was probably correct. This new record, some contended, resulted from the number of undisciplined ideologues that Reagan brought to Washington, the theory being that leaks increase in direct proportion to the ideological content of an administration. Others have argued that it comes from the president's management style: "If every policy is constantly up for a committee decision," said a *Wall Street Journal* editorial, "you are constantly inviting contending parties to fight it out through leaks to the press." Still, all modern presidents, regardless of ideology or other distinguishing features, have complained bitterly about leaks, and it is likely that the record of the each president will fall to the next president as government gets bigger and more complex, as more documents are necessary to produce decisions, as more duplicating machines reproduce documents, and as more reporters look over the government's shoulder. There are no countervailing forces that will realistically shrink the information glut or the access to it.

Some reported leaks have undoubtedly endangered national security, as government claims. But the number must be very small. An evaluation of the suspected national security leaks in the brief period just reviewed is instructive.

—The leak that most infuriated the Pentagon, George Wilson's story of the possible $750 billion budget overrun, was an embarrassment to a cost-conscious administration, but even the assistant secretary of defense had to admit that it did not endanger national security.

—The presence of MIGs in Havana could hardly have been a surprise to the Soviets or the Cubans, and the United States would have to have a low opinion of Soviet intelligence operations to assume that they would be surprised to know that we knew.

—The story on covert actions planned against Nicaragua most closely resembled a consequential security leak. Yet as Georgie Ann Geyer pointed out, the administration's anger was "barely half-hearted," usually a clue that the leak was authorized. Even if that was not the case in this instance, the reaction suggests the administration concluded that the surfacing of this threat would turn out to be in the interest of what the government wished to accomplish.

—When the administration decided to clamp down on leaks of classified information, the only story cited to justify its action, Oberdorfer's report about selling jets to Taiwan irritated the White House because of its diplomatic and political implications; it was not damaging militarily.

Reporters broadcast government secrets all the time, but secrets are produced in government by people with the authority to stamp *Secret* on documents. This has the effect (not always desired in government) of making them more valuable to reporters. Given the generally held opinion that the government is wildly excessive in what it chooses to call a secret—I even saw foreign newspaper clippings that had been classified—a more realistic security classification system, including some penalty for personnel who overclassify documents, would automatically cut down on the number of secrets that get reported in the news media. Government, I contend, is quite good at keeping its real secrets.

To say that government's informal channels of communication actively promote the public good has become a fashionable position in some quarters. "Our particular form of government wouldn't work without it," wrote historian Bruce Catton. Political scientist Richard E. Neustadt has argued that "leaks play . . . a vital role in the functioning of our democracy," and publisher Katharine Graham has claimed they are a "fundamental . . . even necessary, component of our system of government and its communications with the people." Yet a case-by-case study of leaks—even this abbreviated study of a three-month period—shows that they are episodic, flaring up then dying out; they occur for a great many reasons that do not necessarily have anything to do with the public interest; they are never placed in a historical context; and they only conform to the priorities of the person doing the leaking. Neither the reporter nor the government official is thinking of democratic theory when they make their exchange.

Some leaks may promote the public good: the *Washington Post* and *New York Times* stories on the actions planned against Nicaragua offered the opportunities for a full-scale debate on what should be the U.S. role in Central America. Others may injure the public good: the Libyan hit squad leaks ended up with the spectacle of the president of the United States and a minor dictator in a name-calling contest. Leaks qua leaks, then, are not an unalloyed good, although they are a means of protest that is justified for some types of dissenters who do need protection.

To discuss the leaking of information as if it were a rational and necessary system of communicating among Washington players is to assume that those to whom messages are supposedly being sent via the media understand the senders' intentions. If that were so, regular leaks would be a useful way of communicating from one agency to another, from one individual to another within an agency, and from one branch of government to another without having messy confrontations or denials or wasted time and red tape.

Sometimes things do work this way. More often the senders are so clever or so inept as to be totally misunderstood, or else the messages get garbled in transmission. As some of the examples illustrate, there are so many different interpretations of what is being accomplished, by whom, and for what purposes as to seriously call into question the utility and rationality of leaks as an intragovernmental means of communications.

The game, however, does give pleasure to the players. Washington infighting, it is said, is in direct proportion to what is at stake: the stakes are high, hence the leaks. But I think, rather, that the people who are most likely to come to Washington with each political administration bring with them a high talent and tolerance for intrigue. In their previous lives—whether in universities, corporations, foundations, unions, or law firms—this talent probably was manifested privately. Who cared? But political Washington provides the opportunity for public intrigue. Reporters and readers now care, or should. The public ultimately learns more than it would otherwise. Public officials may even act more honorably knowing how hard it would be to keep secret a dishonorable act.

From the point of view of the White House, leaks consistently throw off a president's timing and frame issues in a perspective that is not of his choosing. In political terms a president is fair game; in democratic terms it could be argued that a president should have the opportunity to make his case as effectively as possible, with the opposition then having the same right. In management terms, leaks or the threat of leaks may lead to hurried or conspiratorial decisionmaking. Especially in situations in which presidents have a strong desire to maintain surprise, the lesson they seem to learn in order to avoid leaks is to turn inward: involve the absolute minimum number of advisers in the formulation stage and compartmentalize so that technicians will not know how the pieces are going to be fitted together. The problem, as Jody Powell once pointed out, is that "the damage done by leaks must be carefully balanced against the damage done by excluding people who can contribute to the decisionmaking process."

"How do you cope with leaks?" President Reagan was asked by *U.S. News & World Report* at the end of 1981. "I've been told that you don't," he replied. "Everybody who has been around here for a while tells me it is just the nature of the place." Nearly two years later, on November 23, 1983, the headline across the front page of the *Washington Post* read, "Reagan Ordered Sweeping FBI Probe of Staff for Source of Leak." So to stop leaks, presidents resort to wiretaps and lie detectors. They always fail. In a system of such breathtaking diversity, they always will. Nor is it clear that, on balance, it is in a president's best interest to stop leaks. Is a president more leaked against or leaked for? Most experienced Washington reporters would contend that the answer is obvious. About the investigation reported on November 23, a *Post* headline concluded on December 12, "Justice Probe Fails To Disclose Source of Leak." In the article beneath the headline, reporter Lou Cannon quoted one White House official as saying, "there is no evidence that reporters were told anything we didn't want them to know."

Crisis, Television, and Public Pressure

I n a 1993 speech outlining the Clinton administration's foreign policy, National Security Adviser Anthony Lake cautioned that "public pressure for our humanitarian engagement increasingly may be driven by television images, which can depend in turn on such considerations as where CNN sends its camera crews." This proposition has become the conventional wisdom. And just because it is commonly assumed to be right, it need not be wrong. Yet surely it deserves parsing. We do not respond equally to all stimuli. Could it be possible to make distinctions that can help policymakers gauge how Americans are going to react to images of crisis?

The classic case of a crisis response involves the October 23, 1984, *NBC Nightly News* report about famine in Ethiopia, famine that had gone virtually unrecognized for a decade by American television. Tabulations of what was then seen on U.S. prime-time news programs had shown that the networks had no interest in the African continent other than in South Africa. There were no American network correspondents anywhere near Ethiopia in 1984. When a freelancer offered film on the famine to CBS, NBC, and PBS in 1983, all had turned him down. But the BBC did a story that was seen by NBC's London bureau chief, Joseph Angotti, who urged it

Prepared for a State Department conference, "Multilateral Responses to Humanitarian Crises," October 20, 1993.

on his bosses. They declined. He sent it to New York anyway where anchorman Tom Brokaw insisted on using it.

The response was immediate. A deluge of famine stories followed as viewers pressured the Reagan administration (then in the midst of a presidential election campaign) to respond. U.S. government food aid increased from $23 million for fiscal year 1984 to $98 million, two-thirds of which was committed after the NBC broadcast. But within a year, although famine persisted in Ethiopia, TV coverage had returned to its pre-1984 level. The public had tired of the issue. And the networks, having only discovered Ethiopia by chance, were happy to drop an expensive and unattractive story. Thus ended public pressure on this U.S. policy.

Marvin Kalb, a veteran network diplomatic correspondent who now teaches at Harvard, says that the media have two criteria for covering an overseas event. One: does it have "sizzle"? Does it deal with a riot, a hijacking, or some other happening that can stir emotions? Two: are U.S. troops involved? Famine in Ethiopia had fulfilled only the first criterion. Apparently the first will get a story on the air, but it takes the second to keep it there.

Changes in the TV news business since 1984 also matter. ABC, NBC, and CBS changed hands in 1986, but only one new owner, ABC's Capital Cities, was in the media business. And only ABC remained committed to seriously covering international news. In the cost-cutting world of television networks, a large corps of foreign correspondents, once the pride of CBS and NBC, was replaced by a few parachute journalists. By 1992, for example, NBC had only nine correspondents permanently posted abroad.

Parachute journalism means that the networks pay a great deal of attention to a story, but only briefly. When, on December 8, 1992, the Navy SEALS arrived in Mogadishu and were greeted on the beach by the American media, the three networks together devoted forty-five minutes of prime-time news broadcasts to Somalia. A week later, after the anchormen had gone home, the collective count was down to thirteen minutes; by December 17, it was eight.

These parachutists are exceptional journalists. To watch a Bob Simon or an Allen Pizzey create a first-day story is to watch a master craftsman. Generally, however, parachutists are experts at gathering news, rather than analysts of Somalian or Bosnian affairs. Crises in places such as Moscow, however, are likely to include reportage by resident correspondents who speak Russian, even though they will be muscled aside by their "big feet" colleagues.

The other big news media development since the Ethiopian famine has been the rise of CNN, founded in 1979, but first truly capturing world attention with its Gulf War coverage in 1991. Yet on noncrisis days, CNN has only small audiences at home. While 30 million people in the United States watch the evening news on the three broadcast networks, fewer than a million see CNN's prime evening program. Public pressure is still most likely to arise because of network coverage. (CNN's principal importance in this regard is otherwise. As a twenty-four-hour news service, it is the channel of choice in newsrooms, government agencies, and places where news junkies congregate. Indeed, even presidents watch TV.)

When the TV anchormen left Mogadishu, the networks lost interest in the story. The same happened in Sarajevo; only ABC kept a permanent correspondent, Tony Birtley, in Bosnia during 1992. By the time the spotlight returned to Somalia with the killing of American soldiers in 1993, there were no longer American journalists in residence. The assignment was said to have become unreasonably dangerous. CNN, for instance, had withdrawn Americans after five Somali drivers and bodyguards in clearly marked CNN cars had been gunned down. But the TV people stayed in Bosnia, also a very dangerous posting. A visiting ABC producer had been killed there and the network's resident correspondent had been wounded.

That Bosnia and Somalia appeared to be on a teeter-totter as news stories—when one was up, the other was down—relates directly to Kalb's second law: the cameras follow the troops, or at least go where they expect the troops to be. The added TV coverage from the former Yugoslavia grew out of the expectation that President Clinton was gearing up to involve the United States. The networks began to pay serious attention. Total Bosnian coverage for April 1992 was fourteen minutes; by February 1993 it had risen to ninety-five.

The potential "public pressure" that could have resulted from this new media attention—but did not—is an important part of any analysis of Anthony Lake's proposition about television images. Somalia in 1992 was a searing story of hunger and suffering. Bosnia in 1993 was also about hunger and suffering, and "ethnic cleansing," genocidal impulses, and immense inhumanities. "There is simply no way even to stay alive in the cold," reported Peter Jennings from a hospice in the war zone. "No one comes even to remove the bodies. That is just the way it is. They are freezing to death in Sarajevo." Moreover, it was happening in Europe and was being beamed back to a nation of mostly European ancestry. Still, Americans refused to generate public pressure. (Nor did the United States get involved in Somalia because of television-induced pressure. We were there because George Bush, for many reasons—humanitarian, psychological, geopolitical—willed us to be there.)

What, then, might we conclude from these cases of crisis, television, and public pressure? TV is a reactive medium. It is not in the policy-initiating business, despite what government officials may think. Finding a crisis in Ethiopia was accidental. Overseas camera crews rarely are allowed to go looking for crises. It is too expensive. Other than the episodic sizzle stories, they tend to follow the flag (Somalia) or go into areas of probable involvement (Bosnia).

Thus, a president has great leeway in the period of policy formulation, regardless of television's capacity to generate public pressure. This wide margin for maneuver extends roughly to the point at which American lives are in danger. After that, the TV pictures kick in, and a president's options shrink rapidly.

Foreign Correspondents: The News about Us

The foreign press corps in the United States more than doubled between the mid-1950s and the early 1980s, suggesting that America was increasingly being reported on by reporters of limited experience as America-watchers. By 1982 there were perhaps eight hundred full-time foreign correspondents, almost equally divided between Washington and New York, with a small number on the West Coast. Nearly 40 percent of the Washington correspondents had been in this country for less than three years in 1979; two years later when I resurveyed those who had had less than three years experience in 1979, only 32 percent were still reporting from Washington. This rapid turnover is not accidental. It closely relates to the one-third of all foreign news operations that have a three-year rotation policy.

How long should a reporter stay in a country as large and complicated as the United States? There is a direct correlation between the special problems that the reporters I talked to complained about and the length of time they had been in the United States. The longer they were in residence, the fewer problems.

Based on "Foreign News People," *San Diego Union*, April 4, 1982, and "How Foreign Correspondents Cover the United States," *TransAtlantic Perspectives* (December 1983).

Twenty-three percent, for example, worried about having too much information. This may seem like an odd problem only to those who have never been confronted with mounds of facts as deadline approaches. Too much information can be more debilitating than too little if the reporter lacks the knowledge to select wisely.

There is certainly a daunting, perhaps debilitating, amount of information here. The situation is not a figment of the foreign correspondent's imagination. American reporters may rightly protest any action that appears to limit the flow of news, but what is available looks very impressive to foreigners. As Harold Jackson of the *Manchester Guardian* said, "I think you have the best Official Secrets Act. You simply pour it all out. No one could possibly keep up with it."

Too much information, however, is primarily a problem of the new foreign correspondent. It was cited by 54 percent of the reporters who have been in Washington less than three years, 38 percent who have been here three to five years, 8 percent who have been here five to ten years, and by none with more than ten years' Washington experience.

Longer residency also affects language skills. Reporters from non-English-speaking countries who have been here less than three years are less proficient in English than those who have been here ten years or more.

New foreign correspondents, my survey shows, rely heavily on what they read in the prestige press, especially the *New York Times*. Experienced reporters have much more varied lists of what they consider required reading. They are more hesitant about naming one publication as "most useful" and more apt to respond, "It depends on what's happening." Again, this suggests the fullness of experience.

Eventually foreign correspondents must leave. Noting the problems of staying too long, a Canadian said, "You get stale and start rewriting your stuff. Furthermore, you lose contact with the office and the kind of people you are writing for." Probably a news organization gets value when it keeps a reporter in the United States for five years. If this commitment is too difficult, rotation might be four years, the length of a presidential term. Those who are here shorter periods, as is now often the case, may be misled into believing that Washington is the United States.

In the mid-1950s most foreign correspondents stationed in the United States sent their stories home by mail. Today's systems of instant communication mean not only that the world's press can be more up-to-the-minute, but they also affect what is going to be reported. When foreign correspondents relied on postal services, they were apt to write long analytical pieces that could survive a week in transit. Unable to compete with the U.S. wire services on fast-breaking stories, they made a virtue of necessity while their papers got news of a Senate vote or a plane crash from the Associated Press or United Press. Foreign correspondents now write fewer interpretative pieces and more spot stories. But the movement away from in-depth coverage cannot be entirely attributed to advanced technology. The United States is a major exporter of its concept of journalism, and the brevity, instantaneousness, and multiplicity of events-oriented pieces in our mass media have influenced the way foreign correspondents do their jobs. "This country was a pioneer in TV reporting," a Hungarian reporter noted. "I learned a lot from the media here."

Then, too, competition affects coverage. For many years there were few permanent correspondents from the Middle East in the United States. An Egyptian reporter, recalling his thirty years in this country, said, "Sure it's different now with more Mid-East correspondents. You have to race to compete, to be the first to get the story." He might have wished to take time to reflect, but he knew what his editor would think if a rival scooped him.

Thus a by-product of rapid transmission has been that reporters write more stories each week. The foreign correspondents I surveyed filed a weekly average of eight stories, which was more than their U.S. counterparts. Nearly a quarter wrote ten or more weekly. Technology was clearly pressuring them to produce more. If their organizations were spending all that money to locate them in Washington or New York, they wanted a good return on investment, which was most easily measured in column inches. How could such prolific investigators provide the sort of thoughtful, incisive interpretations that were once the hallmark of the foreign press corps?

Correspondents understand the importance of travel in gaining a balanced perspective of America. "If you travel two hours outside

Washington," said a reporter for a Canadian newspaper chain, "you find people are talking and thinking about things totally unrelated to Washington concerns." But understanding does not automatically translate into plane tickets. Correspondents' travel is limited by budgets and by the nature of foreign reporting, which is largely about what governments are doing. Still, they are a very well traveled group. In 1955 a foreign correspondent averaged half a month a year on the road; by 1979 the average had jumped to thirty-three days.

Charting the trips taken by eighty-seven Washington-based foreign correspondents in 1979 shows that they visited twenty-nine states. But collectively they made ten trips or more to only ten states: in descending order, New York, California, Illinois, Texas, Florida, Pennsylvania, Massachusetts, and Georgia. Georgia was the home state of then-President Carter, and Houston was the communications center for space shots. Texas and Florida are of special interest to Latin America. Increasingly correspondents make an annual trip to California, staying almost exclusively in Los Angeles and San Francisco.

These reporters rarely visited the areas away from the coasts and tended only to go to large cities. Of four trips to Michigan, all were to Detroit; of four to Louisiana, three were to New Orleans; the two to Washington State were to Seattle. According to Tom Littlewood, dean of a journalism school who has written about foreign correspondents, "They don't see and talk to Americans who dine at McDonalds, bowl on Tuesday evenings, attend the stock car races, guzzle beer at Legion halls, or shoot baskets in a ghetto school yard."

Paradoxically, because the institution is unloved by most Americans, it is the presidential nominating system that puts foreign correspondents in touch with noncelebrity Americans. At least once in a four-year cycle they do get to a town meeting in New Hampshire or a farmers' caucus in Iowa.

Foreign correspondents are not the sole source of news for their organizations or even, in most cases, the primary source. Newspapers around the world rely heavily on the wire services, the wholesalers of news. But an organization's correspondents are the Savile Row clothiers of journalism, tailoring made-to-order information for a discrete body of consumers. They can tell their readers, who are usually their own countrymen, how an event personally affects them and can seek out information that might not interest readers in any other country. When General Dynamics Corporation buys the part of Chrysler Corporation that manufacturers the M-1 tank, a Washington correspondent for Zurich's *Tages Anzeiger* tells his readers what the acquisition may mean for the Swiss Army. From Detroit a *Toronto Globe and Mail* reporter explains the split between U.S. and Canadian workers over whether to reopen negotiations with the auto industry.

This is the "home angle," and it was the focus of a study I carried out in 1982 analyzing the space allocated to all U.S.-datelined stories other than sports reports that appeared in sixteen newspapers from nine countries during seven days, February 16–22. Half the papers were published in Western Europe: France (*Le Monde, Le Quotidien de Paris*); the German Federal Republic (*Frankfurter Allgemeine, Sueddeutsche Zeitung*); Britain (the *Daily Telegraph*, the *Times*); and Switzerland (*Neue Zuercher Zeitung, Tages Anzeiger*). Two were from the Eastern bloc: the German Democratic Republic (*Neues Deutschland*); and the Soviet Union (*Pravda*). The remainder came from Canada (*Toronto Globe and Mail, Toronto Star*); India (the *Hindustan Times*, the *Statesman*); and Australia (*Sydney Morning Herald*, the *Australian*).

The researchers divided the U.S.-datelined stories into two categories, those with a home angle and those without, and tabulated the inches of space allotted to each category. From the chart based on the tabulations, it was obvious that the newspapers of different countries had vastly different ideas about their responsibilities to provide readers with a local or regional point of reference.

The German Democratic Republic's *Neues Deutschland*, which ran the fewest home-angle stories, got all its U.S. news from the East German wire service ADN (two reporters in New York, three in Washington). The paper used a lot of very short pieces—averaging fewer than one hundred words—that were clearly rewrites of the U.S. press, presented under such headlines as "Ford Blackmails Workers for Concessions." Twenty-six articles originated from Washington during the week. Two involved Western Europe; none related to or even mentioned the German Democratic Republic.

At the other extreme the correspondents for the Indian newspapers spelled out the home angle in every story. They tended to write

Figure 1. U.S.-Datelined Stories Featuring a Home Angle, by Country

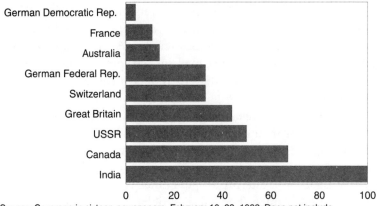

SOURCE: Coverage in sixteen newspapers, February 16–22, 1982. Does not include sports stories.

a few long articles, often between 1,000 and 2,000 words, either on subjects of direct interest ("Indian Scientists Advised to Form 'Brain Bank' ") or else somehow connecting the Indian subcontinent to places as removed from it as El Salvador.

A behind-the-scenes story that delighted British journalists was the reason their papers scored relatively high on the home-angle scale for the week, according to correspondents interviewed. Both British papers reported extensively on the *Washington Post*'s front-page story that reproduced senior staff meeting notes in which U.S. Secretary of State Alexander Haig was quoted as calling the British foreign secretary, Lord Carrington, a "duplicitous bastard." (The lead paragraph in most of the other countries' stories emphasized that Haig's assessment of prospects for peace in the Middle East was grimmer than his public posture.)

In general, though, the European press paid relatively modest attention to the home angle. (For coding purposes our definition was broadly inclusive: a story relating to Europe was coded as home angle even if the correspondent had made no effort to relate the story to his or her own country.) What makes the low percentages doubly perplexing is that the volume of Washington activities involving

Europe was such that *Le Quotidien de Paris* dubbed the period sampled "European Week in Washington."

Prime Minister Wilfried Martens of Belgium (president of the Council of the European Community) received an extraordinary audience with President Reagan to express Common Market concern over the American administration's new budget and the huge deficit it projected. Foreign Affairs Minister Colette Flesch of Luxembourg addressed the National Press Club. British Labourite Wedgwood Benn lectured at the nearby University of Maryland and held a press conference. Italian Foreign Minister Emilio Colombo delivered a speech at Georgetown University in which he proposed a European Communities–United States pact. In addition, the U.S. Chamber of Commerce took a strong stand against those in the Reagan administration who wished to impose economic sanctions aimed at blocking the construction of a Soviet gas pipeline to Europe, the executive council of the AFL-CIO took an equally strong stand in favor of a full trade embargo, and the Joint Economic Committee of Congress released a report on the pipeline project. A U.S. agency, the International Trade Commission, also issued preliminary findings in a case brought by American steelmakers against mostly European suppliers.

Yet collectively these stories were not as attractive to European correspondents in Washington as the president's statements that week on U.S. policy in Central America and the Middle East. Central America generated the most questions at the president's news conference. Mr. Reagan said there were "no plans to send American combat troops into action" in El Salvador or anywhere else, but declined to be drawn into a discussion of options that might be under study. (This followed a *Washington Post* exclusive that asserted the president had approved a plan to encourage paramilitary operations in Central America.) On the Middle East front, news stories that Defense Secretary Caspar Weinberger wished to sell advanced weapons to Jordan caused a public exchange of letters between Mr. Reagan and Israeli Prime Minister Menachem Begin in which the president said, "America's policy toward Israel has not changed."

U.S. relations with two perennially troubled territories dominated not only domestic reportage but also the dispatches of foreign correspondents based in the United States. Editors in such places as Paris, Frankfurt, and Zürich seemed pleased with the "cosmic" dispatches their correspondents filed at the expense of home-angle reporting. Also when I questioned the scarcity of the home angle in conversations with foreign news editors in London and Paris in 1982, their reactions could be characterized as a collective shrug. "Bilateralism isn't much of a story anymore," said a Londoner.

It is hardly ignoble for journalists to want to expand the knowledge of their readers beyond national concerns. Yet I was left with a nagging doubt. Had their distaste for narrow nationalism created a different kind of distortion? This, at least, was the tilt I felt after absorbing 112 newspaper-days of U. S.-datelined stories.

What most of the people of the world know about events beyond their borders will have been told to them by journalists. Even a significant share of what some foreign ministries know will come from the press. Beyond the great issues, then, for each foreign correspondent there should be an additional concern. Formulated as a rhetorical question by a Canadian reporter in Washington, it is, "If we don't report on U.S.-Canadian relations, who will?" Foreign correspondents know the answer; still, part of their special responsibility to their readers is to keep reminding themselves of the question.

Confessions
of a Sound
Bite

As a researcher at a Washington think tank, part of my job is to be helpful to journalists. Consequently, television viewers may have seen me as a sound bite, an oral sentence or two commenting after a presidential speech or before a congressional vote. In 1988 I got 301 calls from American television news operations.

This is what happens. A producer calls to check me out, asking enough questions to know whether I am likely to say what they are after. If I do not respond appropriately, they say they will get back to me. Which means they will not. This is a big city and someone else is sure to have the magic words they are looking for.

It is important to note that they never tell me what to say. This way, they can believe that they are honest journalists. If they choose to interview me on camera, someone shows up and asks a question in as many permutations as it takes to get the answer that is the chip that I am supposed to represent in the mosaic that is their story.

Now, journalism or scholarship usually starts with a hunch or hypothesis. The purpose of reporting or research is to test the hypothesis, find out whether it is true, false, or somewhere in between. If the point of reporting or research is simply to marshal

From the *Washington Post*, October 22, 1989.

facts or quotations to fit a hypothesis, the research or reporting is essentially dishonest. My hypothesis is that television news is increasingly dishonest in that its stories are increasingly gatherings of quotations or other material to fit a hypothesis.

As national and local TV news outlets have come under financial pressure, they have trimmed operations. But smaller staffs mean fewer stories, which means a greater necessity that each assigned story be useable; fewer interviews per story limits the testing of a hypothesis. A researcher who does not gather ten times as much information as he or she can use is probably not much of a researcher. In the TV news business, unfortunately, redundancy is now viewed as a problem to be solved; the goal, apparently, is to gather no more than can be used. As TV news increasingly has no use for information that is not scheduled to fit into a package, it loses interest in anyone who it has determined in advance will not be a sound bite. In other words, reporters tend to interview only those who fit a preconceived notion of what the story will be and a story's hypothesis becomes self-fulfilling.

From time to time a print reporter, usually from a wire service, shops for a quotation. But this is rare. (I base my opinion on hundreds of calls I received from American print reporters last year.) This does not mean that print reporters are more ethical people. Rather, print journalism can still use redundancy. Gathering information is not as expensive. Information not used today may come in handy another day. Even the most otherwise useless interview may yield an enriching detail. And the totality of interviews, used and unused, may be necessary to convince an editor that all bases have been touched.

Television news, it strikes me, is now entering its third phase. In the first phase, the self-conscious period during which print was the dominant medium, a TV story took its hypothesis from the morning newspaper, particularly the *New York Times* in the city where the TV networks are headquartered. TV stories were often illustrated newspaper stories. If the newspaper story from which it was cribbed was correct, the hypothesis did not need to be tested by the TV journalist.

The second phase, which will probably become known as the Golden Age of TV news broadcasting, was dominated by exceptionally experienced correspondents, most of whom had come out of print journalism. Walter Cronkite, David Brinkley, Eric Sevareid, John Chancellor, Daniel Schorr, Bernard and Marvin Kalb, and others offered their news judgments as assurance that a hypothesis was sound, while their prestige within the organization allowed them a good chance to prevail in internal battles.

We now enter, or are about to, a third phase in which increasingly the hypothesis is determined by someone other than the correspondent in the field. Putting together a news story for TV must be a collaborative undertaking, much more so than in newspaper journalism. It is the nature of the technology. As such, there will always be a struggle for control between news gatherers and news processors. What I am now told by network reporters is that the determination of what is news is sliding away from them. This may be even more true at local stations. Kathleen W. Wickham of Memphis State University, who has done site observations at the three network-affiliated TV stations in her city, has concluded that "television reporters . . . initiated almost no story assignments on their own."

Yet the strength of journalism is its vantage point. It may lack insight but at least it sees for itself. A journalism enterprise should question the degree to which it creates a reality warp by moving the power to call the shots too far away from where the shots are fired.

Reporting on States in the American News System

One level of government in the United States gets consistently shortchanged in press coverage. The national media—network television, weekly newsmagazines, and certain elite newspapers—concentrate on international and national news. The local media—television stations and most newspapers—concentrate on city-level news. But news of state government activities too often gets overlooked. This blind spot becomes increasingly serious as the actions of state government become more and more important in our lives.

State governments, unfortunately, often make themselves difficult targets for observation by news organizations and others. Only nineteen of the fifty states have their capitals in their major city. I doubt that most Americans could identify the capitals of Kentucky or Nevada. In some cases—Springfield and Jefferson City, for instance—the capitals were deliberately placed at the center of the state, certainly a justifiable reason, considering the rutted roads of nineteenth century frontier America. Still, Illinois and Missouri state governments would get more attention if their capitals were Chi-

Based on a paper delivered at the conference, "Governmental Structures in the U.S.A. and the Sovereign States of the Former U.S.S.R.," at Hofstra University, April 11, 1992.

cago and St. Louis. The history of siting the seats of government has a certain charm: Tallahassee was chosen, in part, because it was as far away from American Indians and swampland as possible. No state capital was chosen so as to be close to journalists.

But merely relocating the capital would not automatically refocus attention on state government. In 1990 Karl T. Kurtz of the National Conference of State Legislatures contrasted newspaper coverage of legislatures in Colorado and Utah, two Rocky Mountain states with capitals in their principal cities. He faulted coverage in Colorado and praised it in Utah, concluding that the differences were "due to varying civic cultures and the competitive and financial circumstance of the major newspapers."

Another factor that works against creating news bureaus in state capitals, particularly for TV stations, is that many state legislatures are part-time enterprises. Only eight states in 1988 were considered to have full-time legislatures comparable in operational terms to Congress. Seven state legislatures did not even meet in annual sessions.

Local TV news programs also are probably less likely to cover state government if their stations' markets are in more than one state. Maine stations, for instance, also serve the northern part of New Hampshire, and Boston provides most of the television for the state's more populous south.

However, the primary reason why state governments have received less media attention is that they are the most artificial unit of the federal system. Other than the original colonies, a few states with natural boundaries, and the two states that were once independent nations (Texas and Hawaii), most states look like boxes, designed by surveyors and authorized by politicians (which they were). Patriotism is usually defined by nationhood; cities reflect a nation's economic and social being. What of states? I suspect that if you ask a Chicagoan where he is from, he would say Chicago, not Illinois—or Detroit, not Michigan. With only special exceptions (Texans!). In the words of two political scientists, M. Kent Jennings and Harmon Zeigler, "The states are caught between the immediacy of the local system and the glamour and importance of the national and international systems. . . . Too remote to stimulate much participation by their citizens, and too big to make extensive participation possible anyway, these units intermediate between city and nation are probably destined for a kind of limbo of quasi democracy."

The problem with this quite accurate assessment made in 1970 is that things have changed. According to Denis P. Doyle and Terry W. Hartle, writing in 1985, "The last two years have witnessed the greatest and most concentrated surge of educational reform in the nation's history. . . . Indeed, the most surprising aspect of the 'tidal wave of reform' is that it came from state governments." According to Carl E. Van Horn, writing in 1989,

> Important new policy initiatives have come from the states in a broad range of policy areas—natural resources and energy policy, human services and health care, economic development and education, and business and insurance regulation. State governments are deeply engaged in issues that affect state residents on a daily basis—the quality of schools, the supply of water, and the condition of roads and waterways, for example. States are also tackling some of the nation's most difficult problems—surrogate motherhood, the care and treatment of the medically indigent, drug abuse in the public schools, teen-age pregnancy, pay equity, the liability insurance crisis, and the right to die.

And David S. Broder commented in 1992, "Congress and the president have continually laid new responsibilities on the states, while reducing the flow of federal aid. . . . In the current recession, states are making horrendous budget choices—cutting assistance to the poor, choking off support to education, delaying transportation projects, neglecting environmental needs—and raising taxes."

Policy issues, problems being confronted, new responsibilities for states—these are good stories. Surely it is time for American news organizations to reassess the attention they pay to that increasingly significant level of government between nation and city.

A Journalism Sex Test

"The news will not change until the people covering the news change," a reporter in the Washington bureau of the New York Times commented. "If you're going to operate in some wonderland, you can say that your background doesn't color your story," a *Washington Post* reporter added. It makes a difference, according to these newspeople and many readers, whether the news gatherer is male or female, black or white, Native American, Hispanic, or WASP. The composition of the press corps is just one more reason why what you read in newspapers is not objective.

To test this proposition, I challenged my graduate seminar at Harvard. The students—seven women and five men—included a state senator, a university administrator, a radio news editor, a high school teacher, a consumer advocate, and several government officials. A very experienced and savvy group.

They were given four articles—one from the *Wall Street Journal,* one from the *New York Times*, and two from the *Washington Post.* But first I removed the bylines. The students were then asked whether the stories by anonymous reporters had been written by a man or a woman.

From *Columbia Journalism Review* (March–April 1986).

The group voted 9–3 that the *Wall Street Journal* reporter was a man (she was not). Eleven of the twelve thought the *New York Times* reporter was a woman (he was not). They split 7–5 on both *Washington Post* articles. One had been written by a man and the other by a woman. (The majority was wrong in each case.) There was no article for which a majority of the students got the right answer. No student got more than half right; three got them all wrong. Collectively the class received a grade of 29 percent. The men and women earned equally low marks.

How could such an intelligent class have been so wrong? In part, it is because they were too clever by half. They made some choices for reasons other than the text. The *Wall Street Journal* has few women reporters, so the odds were that the article was written by a man. Or a story about male prostitutes in the *Washington Post* would not have been assigned to a woman. The students had grown test wise after years of scenting the traps that professors had set for them in tricky multiple-choice exams.

But they also made interesting assumptions that turned out to be incorrect: that there is a male and female *style* of writing, for instance. Female writing is gushy, the male style titillating. Men are more sensational. Women are more sensitive. The men students were most convinced that sensitive articles were written by women. Otherwise, the main reason the students guessed wrong was that they based their decisions on the reporters' sources. A male reporter, they contended, would not know which feminist business leaders to interview for an article on the romantic involvement of the chairman of the Bendix Corporation with a woman he had promoted to vice president.

One of the students believed that my test was skewed in that all the articles related to issues that had sexist overtones. Thus the reporters must have been particularly on guard against their own prejudices. The results might have been different if I had chosen more run-of-the-mill topics. She may have been right.

My interpretation, however, is that the press reflects where the society is at. In a sense the test is a confirmation of the success of feminism. The students could not correctly detect sexism in these articles because it was not there. This might not have been equally true if we had been looking for other possible biases. One of the stories, for example, was criticized by homosexual groups as being "unfair" and "ignorant." Yet my students and their teacher did not notice this until it was called to our attention.

Looking at four articles in newspapers of high professional standing may not prove anything. Still, this is a do-it-yourself test. Any number can play.

Race, Crime, and the Press

I f the main so-called fact you may still remember from the press accounts of the 1980 shooting of Vernon Jordan is that he was in the company of a white woman, then you and I have something in common even though the fact turned out to be irrelevant as a clue to the identity of the assailant. This would not have surprised Luther Ragin, Jr., who is working for degrees in both law and public policy at Harvard, where I have had the pleasure of teaching him and learning from him. For his instruction and my edification, Ragin wrote a term paper titled "The Treatment of Race in Press Coverage of Criminal Violence." The project involved studying the use or nonuse of racial identifications in the crime stories of Boston's two daily newspapers, the *Globe* and the *Herald American*.

Ragin's first conclusion was that racial identifications appear only when the alleged perpetrator and the victim are of different races. He could find no instances in which newspapers mentioned that attacker and the attacked are of the same race. Yet most crimes are committed by blacks against blacks or whites against whites. By inadvertently giving the impression that violent crimes are typically interracial, newspapers are doing a "grave disservice" to the public, Ragin

From the *Baltimore Sun*, August 4, 1980, and other newspapers.

said. "Violent crimes are typically intraracial; any suggestion to the contrary is not only misleading, but potentially destructive of good race and community relations."

The use of race in a violent crime story, Ragin believed, is justified when it is one of the items of identification that could "facilitate public cooperation in law enforcement efforts . . . (and) could reasonably be expected to lead to an arrest." To illustrate, he presented "Walpole Escaper Sought, May Impersonate Woman," a story from the *Herald American* that begins, "Hey there local girl watchers. That girl you may be watching may not be a girl at all but rather a very bad guy with the very bad habit of carrying hand grenades under his dress." The article never indicates the race of the dangerous female impersonator that the authorities are "on the lookout for."

So Ragin asked fifteen Harvard undergraduates—ten whites and five blacks—what they inferred about the race of the Walpole escaper. All five of the blacks and five of the whites said they thought he was white. ("If he was black, they would have said so.") Five whites thought he was black. ("Most robbers are.") The correct answer is that the Walpole escaper was white. But no thanks to the *Herald American*.

Besides possibly being of help for law enforcement purposes, the disclosure of racial information can be justified, Ragin argued, "when there are compelling reasons to believe that race (or racial animus) is a significant motivating factor in the crime itself." This is when race is a "news value." He cited approvingly the use of race in an article about robberies of elderly white persons by five black men when there was strong evidence that the victims had been chosen because they were white. In many other articles he thought that the references to race were gratuitous.

Please note that I have not identified Ragin's race. Is his reasoning more or less compelling if he is white or black? I also should not have mentioned his student status in that a subliminal reader's reaction might be student equals young equals inexperienced or even unwise. The reference was only bragging on my part since he was *my* student. By the way, I gave him an A+.

Strange that after all these years most newspapers still have not worked out written guidelines to aid their reporters and editors in dealing with this highly sensitive area. Luther Ragin's term paper could help point the way.

Accompanying this essay, the Baltimore Sun *stated that its written guidelines prescribed that proper racial designations were appropriate only:*

—in biographical and announcement articles, particularly when they involve a feat or appointment unusual for members of a particular race;

—when describing a missing person or fugitive, but only when accompanied by a thorough physical description;

—when they provide the reader with a substantial insight into conflicting emotions known to be involved or likely to be involved in a demonstration or similar event. Care should be taken, however, to delineate the extent of racial division or to stress cases in which issues cut across racial lines.

Television
News and
Older
Americans

"There is probably no other identifiable segment of the population, aside from criminals, that is so consistently portrayed in a negative fashion." My student, Michael Dugan, was talking about older Americans, the elderly, senior citizens. He had just spent a week monitoring the local television news in Boston and his findings were the same as those of an earlier national study.

Most TV news stories depict the elderly as first, victims of crime; second, victims of circumstance, such as fire or condominium conversion; or third, recipients of social services, such as hot meal programs. When a story is not negative—"Margaret Hennessey was honored today on her ninetieth birthday by friends and neighbors"—it is slotted into a category labeled human interest. Dugan went to see Mrs. Hennessey. She had been a registered nurse for forty years and was arrested on many occasions in the 1930s for union organizing. She gave her visitor a precise account of what the mayor, governor, and president had or had not done for the elderly during the previous year. She knew the status of bills awaiting action in the state legislature and Congress. But these facts were not in the TV story. The reporter had not asked.

From the *Des Moines Register*, February 4, 1981, and other newspapers.

Dugan concluded, "The one most striking aspect of these types of stories is that we are constantly viewing a group of people having things done to them or for them. These are people who, in effect, have lost control of their lives."

There are exceptions, of course. A researcher at the University of Washington noted that a Seattle station gave more air time to Supreme Court Justice William Douglas's marriage to a woman forty years his junior than it had given to all his judicial opinions combined.

In the stories that Dugan watched, the subjects were always identified by buzz words: *oldster, white-haired, withered, lonely, old-timer.* The camera invariably panned to close-ups of liver spots and wrinkles. The other common denominator that Dugan discovered in the stories was that none of the senior citizens were employed. News about judges, legislators, business executives, or church leaders, however, never refer to the age of the people being covered. Dugan contended that television was "placing a societal value judgment on the worth of people based on whether or not they are still working." He worried that the way TV news stereotypes older people has a profound impact on how the young perceive the old and how the old view themselves.

A 1975 Louis Harris survey reported that older people in larger cities cited fear of crime as their most urgent concern. (Up to that time the top problems had been health or housing.) Yet are the elderly more often the victims of crime? Figures from the Chicago Police Department for 1967–77 show that at no time during those ten years were crimes against the elderly out of proportion to their numbers in the population, and in many parts of the city they were actually underrepresented in being victims. But older people watch television—four to eight hours a week more than other adult age groups—and they "know" that criminals prey on the elderly because they see it on TV all the time. Dugan wondered whether "television created an issue where none existed."

During the past five years there have been many signs that the media are becoming more sensitive to the problems of the elderly and how they are depicted. Helen Hayes appeared in a moving made-for-television film about the trauma of being sent to a nursing home. *Over Easy*, an intelligent program hosted by Hugh Downs, has had a large audience on public TV. Most big-city newspapers have added a regular column, usually once a week, dealing with issues of special interest to older people. Under pressure from the Gray Panthers Media Watch Project, there have been improvements in television advertising and situation comedies.

The area of least improvement, according to Lydia Bragger, who heads the Media Watch Project, is television news. She says that representatives of local and network television are much more receptive to complaints about entertainment TV than they are to those about TV news. Somehow I did not find it very encouraging to learn that the producers of *The Waltons* or a yogurt ad are more responsible and humane than the producers of the *11 O'Clock News*.

Television
News and the
Loss of Place

ncreasingly during the 1980s
Washington became aware of
the potential political impact of
local television news. More
people watch local news than network news. Stations opened
Washington bureaus. A growing tribe of freelancers serviced smaller
stations. Legislators went into the television news business for
themselves, producing electronic press releases and satelliting them
back to their states.

In 1987 and 1988 I asked friends to send me tapes of local
television news from their communities. (My wife claims the exper-
iment was to see how many friends I have. If so, the answer is sixty
hours worth.) My purpose was to better understand how local TV
covers Washington. Eventually I gathered tapes of 106 broadcasts
from 57 stations in 35 cities, ranging in size from Los Angeles to
Grand Junction, Colorado (population 30,000). The tapes were
logged, timed, coded, and run through a computer.

Local newscasts, of course, are an amalgam of news, weather, and
sports. On the 57 stations in my study the average news portion
accounted for 68 percent of the newscast, sports 18 percent, weather
14 percent. This tripartite arrangement differs somewhat according
to market size. News consumed 73 percent of the news program in

The Silha Lecture, University of Minnesota, May 30, 1990.

the top 25 markets, 69 percent in markets 26 through 70, and 60 percent in the smaller markets. The smaller the city, the less news as a percentage of the whole. Also the whole is smaller. Stations in the top 39 markets, New York City through the Greenville-Spartanburg-Asheville region of the Carolinas, averaged 630 minutes of local newscasts each week. Stations in the smallest markets (119 through 208), Montgomery, Alabama, through North Platte, Nebraska, averaged 409 minutes.

There is a higher gloss on newscasts in the large cities, more imaginative camera work, more creative graphics, smoother delivery. This is not surprising. Big stations have larger staffs and more experienced personnel as well as fancier technology. What did surprise me is that content was not essentially different, it just looked better.

My overall impression from watching sixty hours of local news is its sameness. The sameness is not serendipitous. The story of how national consultants in the 1970s created the look, sound, and feel of Action News/Eyewitness News/NewsCenter News has been well told by Edwin Diamond, Ron Powers, and others. Start with upbeat theme music. Build a news set, described by Diamond as "airlines-style reservation counter desks," by Powers as "futuristic, color-coordinated." Design news team costumes. Find anchors who have "rapport" to exchange banter at the commercial breaks—a bit about their personal lives, but not too personal—perhaps comments on their golf game. Add a team character to do weather, sports, or review movies. The TC is allowed to be hairy or even balding.

Anchors increasingly reflect the racial composition of their communities. In a city such as Washington, D.C., it is called a salt-and-pepper anchor team. Yet regardless of race, anchors are meant to leave the same impression, so they look alike. (Which leads to Hess's rule 1: The way to create a color-blind society is to turn the entire populace into TV anchors.) Male anchors do not often have beards, moustaches, or excess poundage. Female anchors do not look old enough for a fifteenth college reunion. Marlene Sanders and Marcia Rock have estimated that a third of local TV news anchors are women, but only 3 percent of them are older than forty, whereas half the men anchors are older than forty and 16 percent are older than fifty.

I listened to local news from stations in Virginia, North Carolina, South Carolina, Georgia, and Florida without hearing an anchor speak with a southern accent. There are also no Baltimore accents in Baltimore, and so forth. (An irony is that you have to listen to national news to catch a good regional accent: the Texas of Jim Lehrer on PBS, the Alabama of Mary Tillotson on CNN, the Tennessee of Fred Graham on Court TV.) Local news comes in two voices: those who report it and those who are reported on. They do not sound alike. The homogenized sound of the broadcasters makes them fungible: one can imagine them with their bags packed, poised to move up to the next market in some other part of the country. This should not give viewers much confidence that these are journalists deeply versed in the culture of their communities. To trace the work history of a successful reporter, such as Paula Zahn of *CBS This Morning*, is to take a quick trip around TV-land: from WBBM-TV (Chicago) to WFAA-TV (Dallas) to KFMB-TV (San Diego) to KPRC-TV (Houston) to WNEV-TV (Boston) to KCBS (Los Angeles). A television career profile can be remarkably similar to that of a professional baseball player: Carolina League to Southern League to triple A before breaking into the majors. Except you do not have to know much local history in order to cover second base for Winston-Salem.

Studies of news directors at local stations show that they too are well traveled. Vernon A. Stone found in 1985 that the typical news director had been in the business for fourteen years and had worked at four stations. His study also showed that the typical director had been in the same job about two years. Six of ten came from other stations. The magazine of the Radio-Television News Directors Association provides a monthly chronicle of personnel changes: "Andy Barton moves to news director at WDSU-TV, New Orleans, from news director, WLKY-TV, Louisville. . . . Mike Crew joins KHTV, Houston, as news director, from news director, KJKS-TV, Jacksonville." Local TV news apparently is a good profession for nomads.

This leads to the central concern of this discussion: More notable than the absence of accent is the absence of place, a sense that this news is special to this locale.

Listening to the five o'clock news for three consecutive nights in October 1987 on Green Bay's WFRV was not a particularly Green

Bay experience. Among the local stories: money-saving tips on how to winterize your home; state senate refuses to create stringent seat belt regulations; two teenagers charged with murder; University of Wisconsin-Green Bay puts condom machines in bathrooms; two-part report on Alzheimer's disease; a man will stand trial for three armed robberies; "Helpline" says be wary of credit clinics; an auto show starts tomorrow; police warn parents to sort through children's Halloween treats; and a "pet saver" report tells how to adopt an animal from the humane society.

Although I heard an automotive reporter on a Detroit station, an Asian affairs reporter on a San Francisco station, and somewhat more agricultural news on one Sacramento station, most of the fifty-seven stations in my study were producing interchangeable parts. (Differences are sometimes most striking in sports, such as ice hockey or curling in Minnesota.)

The formula for a local newscast includes a skimming of world headlines, about 15 percent of the early evening program. On rare occasions a station will ask for comment from an expert in its community: A UCLA professor is interviewed on U.S. activities in the Persian Gulf; a San Francisco priest talks about the pope's visit to the United States. On even rarer occasions a station will relate an outside event to its community: the effect of the October 1987 stock market crash on Atlanta. National and international stories tend to be less governmental or politically oriented than the news one gets from Dan Rather, Tom Brokaw, and Peter Jennings. (An international story I heard on a Detroit station was "The Search for the Loch Ness Monster Continues.")

Compared with the networks, the tone of local news is more titillating: special reports on date rape (Los Angeles) and condom mints (Seattle); tales of an alligator eating a little girl (Pittsburgh) and a boy stuffed in the family's freezer (Atlanta); an item on a state's new obscenity law, illustrated with spicy movie footage (Greenville, South Carolina). Titillation, however, is balanced with public service items—"news to use" as it is sometimes called. How to adopt a baby (Los Angeles), prevent forest fires (Roanoke, Virginia), save water, since "every minute under the shower uses four to six gallons of water" (Seattle), and find the perfect Christmas tree (Grand Junction, Colorado).

During the same period that I was gathering tapes, a conventional characterization of local TV news that was far different from the one I have given dominated journalism journals and the popular press. A *Newsweek* cover story, "The Future of Television," declared:

> The networks' seemingly invincible supremacy over electronic journalism is in jeopardy. Local affiliated stations have suddenly discovered that they don't need the networks anymore to cover the world. With their satellite picture feeds and resource-sharing consortiums, local news operations now have access to virtually any hot spot, be it in Nicaragua or the next state. By the time Rather and Brokaw deliver the story, the folks in Grand Rapids have already seen it all. According to some prophecies, the nightly network newscasters—perhaps the most ritualized manifestation of our teleculture—could be a mere memory by the century's end.

Yet the evidence for such prophecies always seemed to come from the same handful of stations. So in 1986 I asked my research assistant, Deborah Kalb, to interview news directors from 102 stations, a cross-section ranging from large local operations in Philadelphia and Detroit to those in Presque Isle, Maine, and Twin Falls, Idaho. Much to our surprise, they said they were not interested in expanding national and international news coverage. Only three news directors claimed that these nonlocal stories improved their standing in the all-powerful ratings war. The manager of a large Texas station told us, "One thing Washington is full of is talking heads and meetings. These can get boring. . . . Our consultant says government news is boring to viewers." Only once in our sixty hours of watching was an overseas story produced by a station (KING-TV in Seattle did a three-part series on Korea). Statistically, this sort of reporting is so minimal as to confirm the opinion of Lawrence W. Lichty and Douglas Gomery that "local stations cover these stories to build the credibility of anchors and reporters. Virtually all of this effort is for promotional and personal reasons." Predictions that the stations will supersede the networks are going to be wrong. Stations want to be in the *local* news business; everything else is a sidebar. And this is why the loss of place on the local stations is so disturbing. It is not that they want to be someplace else. It is that they do not seem to understand what is so unique about where they are.

The loss of place in TV news is paralleled in TV entertainment. How many people know or care where Roseanne lives? Bob Newhart is not from Vermont, and only the minor characters on *Cheers* speak Boston. After we leave the freeways of the introduction, what does *L.A. Law* have to do with Los Angeles? Must WKRP be in Cincinnati? Hawaii has to look like Hawaii, but there is a separate category for exotica.

Rather, TV entertainment is increasingly about class. *Thirtysomething* is about yuppies. *Bill Cosby* is less about race than about class, the upper-middle; *Married . . . with Children* is about the lower-middle; and *Roseanne* is about what used to be called the working class. What makes this interesting sociologically is that on TV news, as Herbert Gans has pointed out, "class, class groupings, and class differences are . . . rarely reported" unless they are happening abroad to foreigners. Clearly, Americans take their entertainment more seriously than they do their news.

It can be argued that TV news and entertainment TV simply reflect the blotting of regionalism, the blending of all parts of the country. Urban America, after all, is a condition that transcends individual cities, Americans are less likely to spend their entire lives in one location, and changes in communications technologies mean that we now get the same stimuli at the same time regardless of where we reside. As Joshua Meyrowitz has written, "In many ways, electronic media have homogenized places and experiences and have become common denominators that link all of us regardless of status and 'position.'" Nor is this without benefit. Indeed, at a time when other nations seem to be reverting to tribal warfare, such forces that bind a nation together deserve to be promoted.

Still, the case I want to make is based on the belief that Minnesota is different from Maine, that Maine is different from Mississippi, that Mississippi is different from Montana. And that these differences are important to understand and report.

"My wound is geography. It is also my anchorage, my port of call," begins *The Prince of Tides*, Pat Conroy's novel set on a South Carolina sea island. Geography has always been an anchorage for

Americans, even before there was a United States of America. Hector St. Jean de Crèvecoeur, in *Letters from an American Farmer*, first published in 1782, compared the habits of "those who live near the sea," "those who inhabit the middle settlements," and those "near the great woods," concluding, "Whoever traverses the continent must easily observe those strong differences, which will grow more evident in time." Crèvecoeur was better at description than forecasting. Yet nearly 200 years later Carl Carmer would look at the Hudson River and write, "Landscape has an especial influence on those who inhabit it—not merely in economic ways, as the wheat or cotton spring from the earth, not in geographic ways, as rivers and mountains become boundaries to be crossed, but in spiritual and psychic ways."

Since the work of America's first great novelist, James Fenimore Cooper, a sense of place has permeated our literature. Sinclair Lewis had to have been born in Sauk Centre, Minnesota, and Willa Cather had to have grown up in Red Cloud, Nebraska. The poetry of Edgar Lee Masters was shaped by small-town Illinois, just as small-town Maine molded Edwin Arlington Robinson. Even the American writers who were long expatriates—Washington Irving, Edith Wharton, James Baldwin—drew heavily upon their regional roots. Can we imagine the art of Thomas Cole, Albert Bierstadt, Frederick Remington, George Catlin, Winslow Homer, or John Marin except in the context of where they lived? For George Caleb Bingham: life on the Missouri; for Mark Twain: life on the Mississippi. This is not a plea for regionalism. Quite the contrary. Great art uses place to transcend place. Lewis and William Faulkner were Nobel laureates. Art historian Franklin Kelly claims that Frederick Edwin Church produced "the *national* landscape" even while no one would mistake Church's Niagara for the West of Charles Russell.

Nor need we look only at "high culture" and the past. I am a reader of mystery novels and I can assure you that if you want to understand the specialness of Western Pennsylvania, for example, your best guide will be a fictional chief of police named Mario Balzic in the mysteries of K. C. Constantine.

We do not expect this sense of place that is so important to us to be the province of network news. The networks report national events. They use the nation's regions as backdrops for earthquakes, floods, hurricanes, tornadoes, volcanic eruptions; or as the scene of elections for federal offices, unless a state campaign is notably bizarre; or as the locale of certain human drama, such as a little girl trapped in a well. Joseph R. Dominick in the 1970s and Doris A. Graber in the 1980s have studied how network news covers the states and regions. Both found that the Pacific region was the most over-represented and the Midwest the most underrepresented when comparing news time to population. D. Charles Whitney and colleagues at the University of Illinois have pointed out that the overcoverage of large states may in part occur because "the networks have major newsgathering centers there," but whenever a small state gets extensive coverage, it is because of a single story, such as when Klaus von Bülow was tried in Rhode Island.

As for public television, others who understand its convoluted administrative and funding structure far better than I will have to explain the reasons, but it generally gives a cold shoulder to regional news. As Stephen White notes, "the news and public affairs created by the system is almost in its entirety news of national politics and national policy, most of it emanating from the national capital (which is understandably obsessed by such matters)." This national emphasis sharply contrasts with the original intent of the Carnegie Commission on Educational Television whose 1967 report, the motivating force for the present system, wanted public television to be erected "on the bedrock of localism."

Cable TV was also expected to be a narrowcast medium. Indeed, some scholars initially worried that the multitudinous choices it would offer "could conceivably sponsor the ills of fragmentation and faction: members of closed and insular communities talking among themselves but not to outsiders." The choices on cable are there, all right. But they are mostly of old movies, comedy reruns, pop music, stock market readings, home shopping, cartoons, sermons, and sports. In return for the franchise, the locality gets a camera trained on meetings of the city council or county commission.

Even low-power television, the 750 stations in the United States that have only enough transmitting capacity to broadcast in a fifteen- to twenty-five-mile radius, are discovering that the way to profit is to hook up with a network. According to Mark J. Banks of Marquette University, who specializes in LPTV, 65 percent of their programming now comes from networks, and about 30 percent of the stations are operated by owners of more than one station. Typical of the programming offered to low-power stations, a *Wall Street Journal* article comments, is "a pet show in which celebrities talk about their pets."

If low-power TV will not better explain our communities, neither will high-power TV, known as direct broadcast service, the brave new world of satellite dishes the size of dinner napkins that will bring 108 channels of programming directly into our homes. A $1 billion DBS venture was announced in 1990 with four equal partners: NBC, a subsidiary of General Electric; Hughes Communications, a subsidiary of General Motors; Rupert Murdoch's News Corp., owner of 20th Century Fox; and Cablevision Systems Co., also a giant in its field. Clearly these great conglomerates had not joined forces to bring us the local news. Political scientists Jeffrey Abramson, Christopher Arterton, and Gary Orren are on target when they write, "The power of entrenched media giants over the new technologies exposes the fallacy in the technological determinist's claim that the new media are ushering in a golden age of diversity in video programming."

AM radio does sound different in different parts of the country, largely because of call-in talk shows and religious programming. But the more popular FM radio is now almost totally dominated by standard national formats such as country music, adult contemporary, top forty, oldies, and gospel.

The loss of place is not exclusively an electronic phenomenon, of course. Eleanor Randolph of the *Washington Post* wrote,

> Talking about newspapers that are "disconnected" with their communities, [James K.] Batten [chief executive officer of Knight-Ridder] described "newsrooms [that] often are overstocked with journalistic transients. . . . Their eyes are on the next and bigger town, the next rung up the ladder. . . . There is always the temptation to make their byline files a little more glittering at the expense of people and institutions they will never see again."

Weekly newspapers, the backbone of print regionism, are increasingly owned by chains. There are 7,600 weeklies in the United

States. A decade ago 90 percent were owned in the community; today half are chain-owned. Even companies such as Capital Cities/ABC have been buying weeklies. The result, in the opinion of Alex S. Jones, is that "quirky individualism [is] becoming harder to find in dusty weekly offices."

All of which brings me full circle to why the sameness of sixty hours of local TV news is so discouraging. Of all the places from which we can receive television pictures—the networks, public TV, cable, via low-power and direct broadcast service—the only place where we are likely to learn that Minnesota is different from Maine, Mississippi from Montana, is on our local station. This is the one place that can make a healthy profit by stressing the diversity of this nation.

I'm a diversity nut: I am very proud of the fact, the accomplishment, of having spent at least one night in all fifty states. True, I have slept in a lot of hotels that look the same and had meals under golden arches in every section of the country. All is not diversity. Nor will murder and mayhem necessarily look different if they take place in Great Falls instead of Grand Junction. But if we look for what makes our community special, we will find it galore. Just browse through the regional cookbooks in a bookstore. If the ham comes with a choice of gravy, "redeye made with coffee in the dripping or thick white sawmill style made with flour," then you know you're at Aunt Eunice's Country Kitchen on Andrew Jackson Highway in Huntsville, Alabama. And we can view the Statue of Liberty on a New York Harbor cruise that offers kosher dinners. Which brings us to Hess's rule 2: when we can turn on the local news and say to ourselves, "This has to be Tallahassee . . . or Tucson . . . or Twin Falls," then TV will have finally got it right.

Where Journalism Ends and Fiction Begins

n 1993 NBC settled out of court a suit brought by General Motors charging that the network had faked the results of two GM truck crashes. In 1993, too, psychoanalyst Jeffrey Masson initially won a libel suit against Janet Malcolm for her *New Yorker* story profiling him. These two events momentarily focused public attention on where journalism ends and fiction begins.

On November 17, 1992, *Dateline NBC* aired a fifteen-minute segment about the safety of GM pickup trucks manufactured between 1973 and 1987 with the gasoline tanks mounted outside the trucks' frame. Critics contended that this model exploded in side-impact accidents. The NBC program staged two crashes, which culminated in a fifty-six-second scene, a driver's view of the last moments before impact, and a fire that an on-camera safety consultant described as a holocaust. The segment's reporter said that the crash had punctured a hole in the gas tank.

A subsequent investigation by GM proved that the story was fraudulent on five counts. First, NBC had attached remote-controlled model rocket igniters to the trucks. Second, one truck failed to catch fire, and the fire on the other lasted for only fifteen seconds, the filming of which had been enhanced by multiple

From *Responsive Community* (Spring 1994).

camera angles. Third, there was no puncture in the gas tank. Fourth, a previous owner of the truck had lost the gas cap and the gas leakage resulted from an ill-fitting replacement. Fifth, the truck was being driven at speeds faster than were reported on the program.

In an on-air apology on February 9, Jane Pauley told viewers that the incendiary devices were "a bad idea from start to finish." And cohost Stone Phillips added, "unscientific demonstrations should have no place in hard news stories at NBC." GM then dropped its lawsuit and NBC agreed to pay the expenses of the manufacturer's investigation, estimated at $2 million. Media expert Howard Kurtz called it "one of the most embarrassing episodes in modern television history."

NBC later hired outside lawyers to conduct an investigation of what had gone wrong. The report concluded, "Taping a crash fire was at least as important a goal as proving that the GM trucks were defective." The president of NBC, Robert C. Wright, issued his statement: "These journalistic and administrative failures are indefensible."

A more complicated but equally embarrassing incident was a lawsuit by Jeffrey Masson against Janet Malcolm, whose two-part *New Yorker* profile of him had appeared in 1983 after Masson had been dismissed from his curatorial position at the Freud Archives in London. Masson contended that five quotations had been fabricated. In the profile, for instance, he was supposed to have said that he would have turned the Freud Archives into "a place of sex, women, fun."

After a month-long trial, a San Francisco jury found that the five quotations were fabrications and that two of them (including "sex, women, fun") met the three criteria for libel as defined by the Supreme Court: that the quotations were made up or substantially altered, that the plaintiff suffered damages, and that the writer acted deliberately and with "reckless disregard." The jury could not agree on a monetary award.[1]

The trial also delved into Malcolm's writing techniques, notably what she called "compression," or combining quotations from conversations held at different times. In a 1986 deposition, William Shawn, then the editor of the *New Yorker*, said, "This is done frequently for literary reasons. It must never be done to distort

anything or deceive anybody or done to the disadvantage of anybody." But more journalists would agree with *New York Times*
columnist Anna Quindlen: "Grinding up a number of encounters
and molding them into one entity, a kind of journalistic pâté, is
beyond the pale."

Much of the contested material in the Masson profile appeared in
a very long monologue placed at the Chez Panisse restaurant in
Berkeley. Malcolm testified that many of these words had been
spoken over the telephone or in Malcolm's New York kitchen. In
her first draft the scene of the monologue was the Berkeley Pier; it
was shifted indoors by her editor (and husband), Gardner Botsford,
to simplify the story's narrative.

Malcolm's work is part of a continuum of controversial composi-
tions that goes back to the publication in the *New Yorker* of Truman
Capote's *In Cold Blood*. That mid–1960s, real-life story of the murder
of a Kansas family employed all the techniques of fiction while
claiming to be "immaculately factual." But how factual can quotations be when the reporter did not hear them? The same question
was raised about *The Final Days*, a 1976 book about President Nixon
by Bob Woodward and Carl Bernstein. And in 1984 *New Yorker*
writer Alastair Reid, obviating such a question, admitted that his
reporting was a distillation of things he had seen and heard in
different places. Reid, and perhaps the others, were imposing their
wills on events and other people's words "to make [in Reid's
judgment] the larger truth."

Which brings us back to NBC's setting fire to a GM truck. Is this
incident merely an aberration, a dishonest moment on a news
medium that otherwise conforms to the standards of mainstream
print journalism? Is it proof that TV news is intellectually dishonest,
a massing of sound bites and pictures in support of predetermined
conclusions? Is it proof that the image-based journalism of television
is creating a different standard of truth? It is all three.

The television newsmagazine format is now so popular and profitable that it is even beginning to dominate prime-time programming. At the same time, the newsmagazines have become the
driving force of the networks' news divisions, affecting decisions on
personnel and resources. Their influence on dinnertime news pro-

grams—still watched every evening by 30 million people in the United States—is also evident from the increased use of features with names such as "American Agenda" and "Eye on America," which borrow newsmagazine techniques.

The TV newsmagazine was born on September 24, 1968, when the news division of CBS first aired a topical prime-time show called *60 Minutes*. By 1979 *60 Minutes* was the most widely viewed program in the nation. According to its executive producer, Don Hewitt, it was "the biggest moneymaker in the history of broadcasting," having earned $1 billion for CBS—clearly worth imitating. By 1993 ABC, CBS, and NBC were producing seven newsmagazines and had at least three more in the pipeline. And in 1987 Rupert Murdoch's Fox stations had introduced *A Current Affair*, a highly sensationalist newsmagazine that was also imitated by other syndicated programs.

The mid-1980s was a period of flux in the television industry. Murdoch was laying plans to create a fourth network, and the three major networks were changing hands: ABC was acquired by Capital Cities; Loews bought 25 percent of CBS and made investor Lawrence Tisch its president; General Electric replaced RCA as the parent company of NBC. The networks had always viewed their news operations as loss leaders, good public relations for a government-regulated industry. But times were tough, and the new corporate owners were offended by waste and redundancy. Soon, Dan Rather was publicly scolding his new bosses on the op-ed page of the *New York Times*: "Do the owners and officers of the new CBS see news as a trust . . . or only as a business venture?" As anchor, however, he was only entitled to the next-to-last word. The new owners wanted—and got—scaled-down news operations, and they substituted newsmagazines, which were cheap and network owned, for dramas and sitcoms, which were expensive and owned by others.

Don Hewitt's newsmagazine format transformed the journalist from an objective observer into a Dick Tracy-like protagonist: reporter-detective outlines the case, searches for clues, stalks the transgressor (often a corporation or a government agency), and, if possible, brings the perpetrator to justice. Reporter-detective, especially if played by Mike Wallace, even wears a trench coat, and, according to media scholar Richard Campbell, "may appear in as many as 40 or 50 shots in a 120-shot, 14-minute segment."

Just as Capote drew on the conventions of fiction in his nonfiction novel, Hewitt and his disciples adopted the techniques of Hollywood screen imaging. Villains are shown in extreme close-up. (Extreme villains, such as the Shah of Iran, have both forehead and chin cut from the frame, while middling villains usually just lose the tops of their heads.) The reporter-detective, however, is seen from a distance.

Hidden camera investigations, often with reporters operating in disguise, have become another staple, especially on ABC's *Prime Time Live*, whose executive producer has said he would like to do a hidden camera story every week. "Journalistic practices that would get you fired from the *Chicago Tribune* or the *New York Times*—surreptitious eavesdropping or assuming a false identity—are standard techniques on the CBS program *60 Minutes* and similar shows," lamented Richard Harwood, a former ombudsman of the *Washington Post*.

Other techniques used at various times, in hard news shows as well as newsmagazines, include simulation of events by actors, music to heighten mood, changes in sequencing, fast cutting that reduces sound bites to a sentence, generic images for illustrative purposes, weighted expert opinions, and ambush interviews. There are many examples:

—ABC's *World News Tonight* used an employee to play an American diplomat handing a briefcase to a Soviet agent.

—*CBS Evening News* used a rap music video of President Bush repeating "read my lips" to synthesizer accompaniment.

—Ted Koppel's *Nightline*, during an interview with a juror on the Rodney King trial, used music that TV critic John Carmody described as an "almost ominous chord—faintly reminiscent of the note sounded when Rick sees Ilsa for the first time since Paris."

—*NBC Nightly News* used images of dead fish to illustrate a 1993 story about alleged overcutting in Idaho's Clearwater National Forest. The fish turned out to be neither dead nor from Clearwater, and Tom Brokaw apologized on a later broadcast.

—An animal rights segment on *60 Minutes* had a five-to-one ratio of expert opinion in favor of one side, according to the count of one media critic.

Balance is clearly not the objective. The producer of CNN's *Network Earth* series said, "Indeed, [balance] can be debilitating. Can we really afford to wait for our audiences to come to [their] own conclusions? I think not." The objective is usually a sting, which is why ambush interviews are so effective. Interviews in which a trapped suspect refuses to answer the reporter-detective's questions serve simultaneously to underline the target's guilt (Why else wouldn't he talk?) and create an illusion of fairness and balance (he was given the chance, after all).

Is the fire on *Dateline NBC* an indicator of dishonesty in TV news? Clearly, when the program's producers arranged to make certain that a GM truck would explode, they violated the network's written policy: "If it isn't happening, you cannot make it happen. Make no effort to change or dramatize what is happening." Still, when the *New York Times*, *New York Daily News*, *Washington Post*, *USA Today*, and *New Yorker* had similar problems with fabrications, the journalism community regarded them as having harbored a sloppy editor or a bent reporter, not of being innately dishonest. The NBC incident, at one level, should be viewed as a similar aberration.

On another level the breach of standards at NBC is more than a blip on journalism's ethical echocardiogram. Increasing institutional pressures in the news business—particularly in television—to cut ethical corners make hoaxes like NBC's much more likely. TV videotape is, for example, increasingly coming from freelancers, syndicates, amateurs who happen upon a scene, and groups trying to interest TV programs in their points of view—in short, from people whose credibility and news judgment are questionable. In 1986 ABC and NBC purchased and aired a videotape that purported to show the nuclear meltdown at Chernobyl but turned out to be of a cement factory in Trieste, Italy.

Even if NBC's truck segment was an aberration, it still illustrates that TV news is intellectually dishonest. The newsmagazine report was designed to *show* that the trucks were defective, not to *test* whether the trucks were defective. All journalists start with a hunch. The purpose of reporting should be to test these hunches. When reporters simply marshal facts, quotations, or pictures to support their hypotheses, they sell out their mission, an argument I have made in the essay, "Confessions of a Sound Bite," in this book.

As the TV news industry has trimmed operations, smaller staffs increasingly need each assigned story to be usable. Moreover, fewer interviews and less time per story both limit the testing of a hypothesis. Redundancy is now viewed as a problem rather than as a rigorous method to be prized: reporters seek to gather no more information than a story can use. TV news now has no interest in the complexities of a story if it does not mesh with the producers' preconceived notion of what that story will be. Inevitably then, the story's hypotheses are self-fulfilling.

TV news began as an illustration of events, not unlike a courtroom sketch. The fictions of presentation, such as the reverse-question technique in which the interviewee's answers and the interviewer's reactions are filmed separately, were modest. TV journalists generally stuck to the standards of print reporting.

Times have changed. Indeed, as the newsmagazines increasingly place journalists in prime time, their success will be measured by showbusiness standards. An irate professor at the Columbia School of Journalism wrote in the *Wall Street Journal* after the NBC-GM controversy that "TV 'news' is today increasingly peopled with 'journalists' who are often little more than actors playing the role of journalist." Although the comment slights some very competent people, it is likely that their most valuable on-camera skills have nothing to do with news gathering. As Everette Dennis has pointed out, poll data show that "many respondents could not tell the difference between serious evening news programs, talk shows, and programs that use a news format but which are designed to titillate and entertain."

TV's image-based journalism is a conveyor of information through moving pictures, and as such, its truth must be filmed. That is why it was so important to the *Dateline NBC* producers to set the truck on fire. This different standard will become more pronounced as the older generation of TV journalists, who learned their craft on newspapers or wire services, leave the scene. The "new news," as it is already called by advocates, suggests a brave new future for the world of television reporting. Stretched by the potential of filmmaking, it seeks to adjust truth to incorporate and accept changing frame space, rearranging sequences, fast cutting, adding music, even reenacting events: the larger truth, it will be claimed, truth in spirit if not in detail. And perhaps then, as Richard Reeves has noted, "Situations such as the pickup truck scandal are going to happen again and again, and each time it will seem less important, as fact and filmmaking merge into a new, nonlinear information form." Is it too late to relearn a lesson from novelist and journalist John Hersey? In the autumn of 1980 he bluntly stated the case: "The writer of fiction must invent. The journalist must not invent."

Note

1. In November 1994 at a retrial of the Malcolm-Masson case, the jury declared against the psychoanalyst, concluding that although two quotations in the *New Yorker* article were false and one was defamatory, none was written with the recklessness required for a finding of libel.

Index